VIRGINIA
Q·U·I·L·T
MUSEUM

TEXT BY JOAN KNIGHT

PHOTOGRAPHY BY POLLY FRYE

HOWELL PRESS
Charlottesville, Virginia

Designed by Lisa Wayand
Edited by Meghan M. Mitchell

Library of Congress Cataloging-in-Publication

Knight, Joan.
    Virginia Quilt Museum/Joan Knight; photography by Polly Frye.
            p. cm.
Includes index.
ISBN 1-57427-105-9 (pbk.)
        1. Quilts—United States—Catalogs. 2. Quilts—Harrisonburg—Catalogs.
        3. Virginia Quilt Museum—Catalogs. I. Frye, Polly. II. Title.

    NK9112.K59 2000
    746.46'074755'922—dc21

                        00-040776

            ISBN 1-57427-105-9
            Printed in Thailand

11 10 09 08 07 06 05 04 03 02   10 9 8 7 6 5 4 3 2 1

            Published by Howell Press
            1713-2D Allied Lane
            Charlottesville, VA 22903
            (434) 977-4006
            http://www.howellpress.com

•CONTENTS•

•CONTENTS•

· P R E F A C E ·

WHEN THE VIRGINIA QUILT MUSEUM opened on August 25, 1995, its permanent collection consisted of fifteen quilts. Through the generosity of donors and sponsors the collection has grown to include more than eighty-five pieces. Each quilt is an important part of our quilting heritage, and each has its own story to tell, but for practical purposes only part of the collection can be presented here. Therefore, a variety of quilt styles has been selected for the reader's enjoyment. Let the quilts speak to you. Enjoy their stories, and delight in the beauty of their colors and designs. Learn from the quilt-making techniques represented. Then, you will understand the importance of the museum's mission: to preserve our quilting heritage and promote the continued practice of quilt making.

The Virginia Quilt Museum's schedule includes three exhibitions per year. Quilts from the permanent collection are displayed on a rotating basis, as space permits, during each exhibit.

Joan Knight
Director/Curator

·ACKNOWLEDGMENTS·

THE VIRGINIA QUILT MUSEUM wishes to express its gratitude to the individuals and organizations that have donated quilts or sponsored their purchase for the museum's collection. By preserving part of our quilting heritage for generations to come, through their gifts they have made history. Our sincere thanks to:

Eleanor B. Allen, Mrs. Josephine Barber, Mrs. Lonnah Billings, Mr. and Mrs. Beverly Bowers, Mr. and Mrs. William S. Brown, Eleanor J. Burleson, James Faulkner Channing, Cheri Clum, Ruth H. Cone, Cathy Crocker, Janet B. Downs, Mary Elliott, Mary Spitzer Etter, Mrs. Basil Gray, Nancy Gillis, Mrs. Julia Grandle, Mary Ware Greene, Terry and Paula Golden, Merlyn Hunger, Carter Houck, Barbara Hutchens, Dorothy A. Jarmoska, Dr. and Mrs. Thomas P. Keenan, Kernstown United Methodist Church, Jean Knowlton, Mildred Lee, Mr. and Mrs. Charles M. Leigh, Pauline Liggett, Ruth Farley Massey, Geneva Funk McClung, Diane Leonard Messick, Judy and Merle Meyer, Anne Morgan, Sylvia S. Moore, Mr. and Mrs. J. Matthews Neale Sr., Louise Nichols, Ann Ober, Lee and Lynn Perry, Sue Poe, Questers - Robert E. Lee Chapter #60, Dorothy Reid, Neves Robinson, Le Rowell, Thelma Shirley (The Little Shop), Sandra Sider, Stephens City United Methodist Church, Ruth Thompson, Charlotte Veregge, Jane Walrond, Sarah Watkins, Julia Wernicke, and Gordon Whitacre.

Cabin Branch Quilters Guild, Cardinal Quilters Guild, Country School Quilters Guild, Madison County Quilters Guild, Piecemakers Quilt Guild, Shenandoah Valley Quilters Guild, Skyline Quilters Guild, Waterford Quilters Guild, Quilters Unlimited of Northern Virginia, and the Virginia Consortium of Quilters.

Thanks also to:
Carter Houck, Nina Naruszewicz, Wilsene Scott, and Judy Stryker, for hours given to conservation work and the application of sleeves to the backs of the quilts, as well as for days spent assisting with photographing the collection. Thanks also to Thea Weeks, who photographed the quilts in black and white for our files.

Polly Frye, for time and talent given to photographing the quilts for the book, thereby providing the museum with a visual record of its collection.

The volunteers and board members whose appreciation of and interest in quilt making and continued support make it possible for the museum to operate from day to day.

Our publisher, Ross Howell, for his interest in the Virginia Quilt Museum. His patience, guidance, and encouragement in the preparation of this book are much appreciated.

Meghan Mitchell, for her expertise as our editor. She came to know quilting terms, pattern names, quilt makers and their stories along the way, putting them all together as only she could do and guiding our every step to make this book a reality.

·INTRODUCTION·

MANY GREAT IDEAS and great dreams disappear; many founder on the rocks of indecision and ennui. If, instead, an idea goes on to maturity and proves to be as great as it sounded, the forces that drove its realization may never be apparent to the many people who later say, "What a great idea!" Fortunately, once the idea takes shape and starts to grow, many inspired enthusiasts often follow the lead, help to form the finished project, and continue to move it ahead. The Virginia Quilt Museum, brainchild of Joan Knight and Suzi Williams, owes its existence to an entire community of quilters and civic-minded citizens.

In January 1991, after a particularly successful teaching session at Belle Grove Plantation, Joan Knight and Suzi Williams had a great inspiration—"Wouldn't it be wonderful to have a permanent quilt museum in Virginia?" It's hard to say who first expressed the idea, but it immediately seemed to both Joan and Suzi that it was a foregone conclusion, so they made a proposal to the Belle Grove board of directors, whose members found it tantalizing.

It was not long before the Virginia Consortium of Quilters had given seed money, a logo had been designed by an artist under the guidance of Jackie Kellam, and lawyer Bruce Mayer had guided them through the necessary maze of legal incorporation. The year was 1992, and four people were asked to be board members and agreed to serve. They were Ellen Banker, Anna Holland, and the two pioneers, Joan Knight and Suzi Williams. They were joined by two consultants, Colleen Callahan of the Valentine Museum in Richmond and Gary Barrow, Virginia folklife coordinator.

By August 1, 1993, a complete board was in place. Among its members were people with many necessary talents, from finance and publicity to building and acquisitions.

Along the way money has been made in the way quilters know best—by raffling off quilts and other handcrafted items. Local papers and national publications have been generous with articles, notices, and announcements. Of course, just as in the nineteenth century, word of mouth has proved to be the way quilters work best! The collection started to grow even before there was a building to house it.

Early on, there was a nebulous plan to build a separate building at Belle Grove—but the amount of money needed became ever more staggering. It was decided to seek an interim location that had an existing building. Then, in one of those fortuitous turns of fate, the lovely nineteenth-century Warren-Sipe House (in downtown Harrisonburg and with a huge municipal parking lot just behind) became vacant. The property belonged to the city of Harrisonburg, and city officials agreed to let the museum use the house at rock-bottom rent. A summer of scraping, scrubbing, and painting by interested volunteers in 1995 readied the site for its opening in late August.

Rooms with grand fireplaces and a beautiful staircase, to say nothing of the lavatory, kitchen, and large, secure storage space, make it possible to hang shows in a variety of ways and to accommodate workers, visitors, and, most importantly, the ever-growing collection. The second floor has space and light for more display as well as a library, classrooms, and an office. Two smaller rooms on the first floor allow for a desk for the day's volunteer (or anyone who needs it) and a well-stocked shop.

Gradually, the museum has grown easily into the attractive old house. Wheelchair accessibility has been added and various other building codes met. The city of Harrisonburg has expressed its desire to turn the house over entirely to the museum in its fifth year. Once the building becomes the permanent location, there will be a drive toward modernized air conditioning and other amenities. As the dream has neared reality, the museum has received more and more gifts of terrific quilts, as well as money to purchase others that fill special needs in the collection. The lack of a limit on the time period of quilts acquired has sped growth.

Many loyal supporters of the museum who cannot put in time working there have run fund-raisers and publicized the museum and its needs as they travel. Jinny Beyer has opened her wonderful "quilt garden" to throngs of admirers, serving them tea and cookies—all to raise money for the museum. Classes and lectures, as well as such fund-raising events as auctions and fashion shows, are ever popular with members and first-timers alike.

The museum is community- and user-friendly—reaching out to meet many needs. Bus tours can be scheduled, and guidance is provided for museumgoers who are just beginning to discover quilts. When there is a citywide celebration, such as the New Year's Eve "First Night," you can be sure the museum is open and welcoming. Information and artifacts are interchanged with other museums. Students from the local college, James Madison University, can use the museum as a resource for writing courses or the study of textiles. In a very short time, this small museum in the large Victorian house has become not only well known but important to its community and to the state.

It is impossible to list the names of every person who has donated time, money, and ideas to the growth of the Virginia Quilt Museum, but a huge and heartfelt THANKS goes out to all of the museum's friends. For giving the quilts that started the museum's permanent collection, deepest gratitude is extended to each of the quilt donors.

Carter Houck
VQM Board of Directors

THE WARREN-SIPE HOUSE

HOME OF THE VIRGINIA QUILT MUSEUM

LOCATED IN THE HEART OF the Shenandoah Valley, the quilt museum makes its home in the historic Warren-Sipe House in downtown Harrisonburg. Edward Tiffin Harrison Warren, a direct descendent of the city's founder, Thomas Harrison, contracted to have the house built about the time of his marriage to Virginia Magruder in 1855. Some say it was a wedding gift. Completed in 1856, the building is a grand brick structure with large rooms, twelve-foot-high ceilings, and a lovely center hall staircase.

Warren rose to the rank of colonel during the Civil War and served in the 10th Virginia Volunteer Infantry Regulars. In May 1864 he was killed at the Battle of the Wilderness. It is said that his ghost, clad in full uniform and with sword and bandaged head, sometimes appears at the top of the stairs. Some say he silently peers down the steps; others say he slowly descends the staircase. Years after Warren's death, his wife sold their home.

In 1894, Mr. George E. Sipe purchased the house. He was a prominent attorney, civic leader, and member of the House of Delegates. Mr. Sipe added an attic to the original structure and the kitchen to the rear of the building. His most admired additions are the carved mahogany fireplace frames, one featuring cherubs and the other a floral wreath, and the inlaid wooden floors on the first floor. Both architectural features inspire visitors to create quilting patterns from their designs.

In 1956, the city of Harrisonburg acquired the house. It was used for many years as the recreation department, serving 120 children per day and hosting many lively community dances. The Harrisonburg-Rockingham Historical Society took up residence in the house in 1978 and remained there until the early 1990s.

Just prior to the city's offering to lease the house to the quilt museum, court was held in the building while the courthouse on the square a few blocks away was being renovated. During that period a holding cell was installed on the first floor for prisoners waiting to come before the judge. Since the museum opened its doors in August 1995, the "jail" has provided secure storage for the museum's quilts, as well as a curiosity for visitors.

The structure has been sparkled up both inside and out. The city of Harrisonburg generously underwrote the cost of the installation of the wheelchair ramp, repairs to the roof, and the painting of the building's exterior. Community businesses have made numerous donations, and volunteers have contributed thousands of hours to the renovation, refurbishing, and operation of the museum.

Thus, a dream has become a reality. The grand old house is now the Virginia Quilt Museum, preserving our quilting heritage.

CHINTZ CENTER MEDALLION QUILT
c. 1810   108" x 109"

This is the oldest quilt in the museum's collection. Its center, appliquéd and surrounded by chintz borders, is typical of Virginia and Maryland quilts of the era.

The quilt maker, Jane Weakley Leche (1794–1855), was born in Pennsylvania, married David Leche in 1819, and then moved to Baltimore. She made this quilt prior to her marriage. Using two different fabrics for her appliqué work, Jane created a tree of life medallion design for the center. A fountain is pictured within the tree motif, and two butterflies cut from fabric are sewn to the upper corners of the block. The center of the quilt is surrounded by pieced triangles edged with a triple border consisting of two single chintz strips on either side of a wide pieced strip. Cross-

hatching and straight lines were used to quilt the piece.

From the donor's handwritten notes, which accompanied the quilt, we learn that Jane Leche "was of medium size (about 130 lbs.), had hazel eyes, and very beautiful dark brown hair. She was very devoted to her children and a good housekeeper. She did all kinds of fancy-work and embroidery. She used also to keep a regular set of tools and amused herself by making shoes for little children. She was a very clever woman. She also possessed a sweet voice and sang well, being accustomed to hum while at her work. She was possessed of a cheerful disposition. Her home was at the southwest corner of Charles and Fayette Streets, Baltimore, Md."

Jane's daughter Elizabeth Eleanor Leche married into the Crawford family of Runnimede in Woodstock, Virginia. Elizabeth's daughter Eleanor Crawford Jackson inherited the quilt and gave it in turn to her daughter, Eleanor Jackson Burleson, who gave it to the museum in honor of her mother and her aunt.

Gift of Eleanor Jackson Burleson

STAR OF BETHLEHEM QUILT
1827   99" x 96"

Known as the Star of Bethlehem or Carpenter's Wheel, this quilt was made in Rockingham County, Virginia, in 1827. The quilt maker, Abigail Lincoln Coffman (1801–1882), was related to Abraham Lincoln's father, who was born in the county. History tells us that she was a woman of strong will, as reflected by the large name and date stitched onto her quilt. Double lines of quilting stitches spell out "Abigail Coffman" and "1827" near the center of the lower edge. It is very unusual to find this type of identification on such an early quilt.

In *The Lincolns in Virginia*, historian John Wayland reports that Abigail wanted to

marry the brother of her sister's husband. Abigail's father, however, did not want to have two sons-in-law from the same family, so he chose another young man, Mr. Joseph Coffman, for her. Abigail objected, and her father locked her in an upstairs room in the family home with only bread and water until she changed her mind. Wayland writes, "It is doubtful whether she ever did come around to his way of thinking, but she finally agreed to marry Joseph Coffman and married they were on October 6, 1818. She remarked to her bridesmaids, when they were helping her put on her veil, that she would rather be dressing for her funeral."

Abigail made this quilt nine years after marrying. It is hand pieced. Diamond shapes form a ring around an eight-pointed star at the center of each sixteen-inch block. She chose to use shades of pink, brown, and blue cotton fabrics. The quilting includes cross-hatching and straight lines; four lines are visible in the alternate blocks, and double lines appear in the pieced blocks. Eagles are quilted in the corners, and a small tulip motif can be found over the top of the quilted date.

A border of diamonds in a zigzag pattern frames the quilt. A small eighth-inch binding was formed by bringing the backing to the front, forming the finished edges.

Like the quilt, Abigail and Joseph's house still exists today, near Cook's Creek in Dayton, Virginia.

VQM purchase

Julie Anne Faulkner in 1864, when she was forty-three years old.

CROSSED LAUREL LEAVES
c. 1836   97" x 80"

According to family history, this quilt was made by Julie Anne Frederick of Frederick County, Virginia, for her marriage to Isaac Hamilton Faulkner in November 1837. The bride's family was of German descent and observed the custom of the dowry, by which the bride provided the linens for the bedding of her new home and the groom provided the furniture.

Julie Anne's quilt is made up of twenty fifteen-and-a-half-inch blocks that were appliquéd using indigo blue and salmon pink cotton fabrics on an off-white background. The design consists of crossed stems, each lined with six indigo leaves. Three salmon-colored leaves were sewn at the tip of each stem to resemble a tulip. Beautiful hand quilting outlines the appliquéd shapes, and echo quilting is used in some areas. The border features a mean-dering feather swag; small, quarter-inch-spaced straight lines fill the background.

Within the Faulkner family, the quilt is known as the Tulip Quilt.

As the wife of a Winchester, Virginia, merchant, Julie Anne spent the Civil War years at her residence on Water Street. She had four sons, all of whom served in the Confederate army. One of the sons, James Frederick Faulkner, the grandfather of the quilt donor, was a member of the Stonewall Brigade. In 1863 he was captured at the Battle of Chancellorsville and imprisoned at the infamous Camp Chase in Columbus, Ohio. He was released and returned to Virginia to become one of Mosby's Rangers, serving until the end of the war.

Gift of James Faulkner Channing

HEXAGON MOSAIC QUILT
c. 1830—60   100" x 104 ¹/2"

This quilt features pieced hexagon mosaics sewn with a variety of period fabrics, several of which are block prints exemplifying the use of blue overdyed with yellow to create green. The top consists of three muslin strips appliquéd with six-inch mosaics. A 7 ¹/2"-wide floral print border frames the quilt, and a handmade fringe two inches wide is sewn along three sides and a section of the fourth. It is not known whether the quilt maker ran out of fringe on the last side or whether part of it came loose and was discarded.

The mosaics are outline quilted, and the remainder of the piece's background is quilted in a zigzag pattern.

Gift of Ann Ober and Mary Elliott in memory of Kathleen Davis Addison

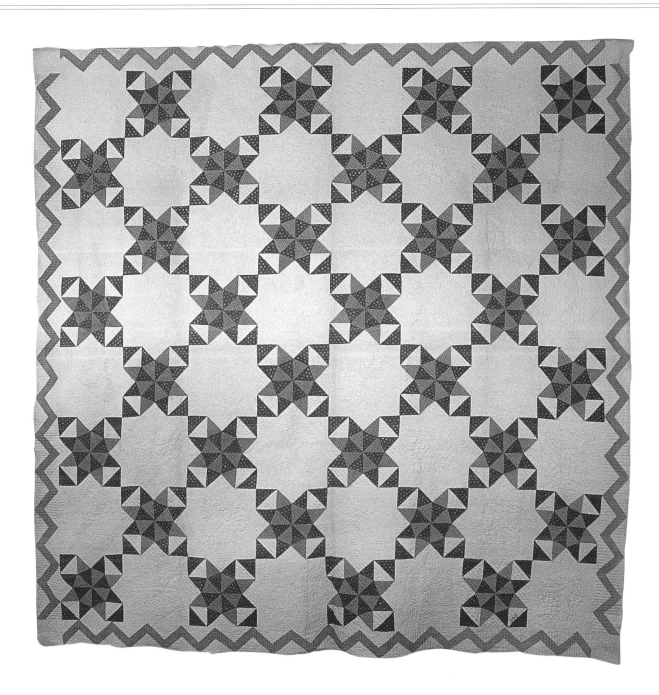

MORNING STAR QUILT
c. 1840   93" x 93"

This quilt comprises thirty-two pieced blocks set with plain alternate blocks. It is distinguished by its very fine quilting: straight lines in the pieced blocks, and a grape cluster and leafed vine in each of the alternate blocks. The border is a zigzag or Streak of Lightning pattern, a design frequently found on old Shenandoah Valley quilts. The quilt maker is unknown.

Gift of Ruth Farley Massey

STRIPPY CRIB QUILT

c. 1840 45" x 44"

Made of high-quality cotton, this quilt is designed in lengthwise strips of pink-and-white print, blue print, and plain white fabric. The zigzag, or Streak of Lightning, pattern is found often on early Shenandoah Valley quilts. The piece was quilted in straight lines, waves, and triangular shapes.

Over the years, the corners of the Strippy Crib Quilt have been torn away, but the fine needlework of its maker can still be appreciated. Conservation work has been done on the piece to stabilize it. The fact that it is a strippy quilt, as well as its age, makes this a rare find in children's quilts.

Sewn to its bottom edge are two pieces of twill tape, probably used to tie the quilt to the crib.

Gift of Ruth Farley Massey

LUCINDA'S DOLL QUILT AND THE CRAZY PATCHWORK FISH
c. 1840 and c. 1900   4 1/2" x 4 3/4"

The smallest quilt in the museum's collection was made by Lucinda Robinson Rice (1835–1919), who was born in Roanoke County, Virginia. Lucinda was a young girl when her parents decided to join relatives from the Shenandoah Valley and go west by Conestoga wagon to settle on the prairie. The family traveled as far as Illinois and founded the town of Virginia, just west of Springfield.

Lucinda was five years old when she made the little doll quilt. Hand stitched, it is made up of five tiny pieced eight-pointed star blocks, each 1 3/8" square, set with alternate blocks of rosebud-printed fabric. The quilt is backed in white-and-gold print fabric; a brown-striped fabric was used for the binding.

It is hard to imagine young fingers making such a small quilt, but one has to remember that girls were taught to sew at a

very early age in the 1800s, and some were quite proficient by the age of five.

As Lucinda grew up, she often returned to Virginia to visit relatives in the New Market area. It was on one such visit that she met her husband-to-be, Dr. F. E. Rice, a prominent physician. They lived their entire married life in New Market. Lucinda wrote her memories of the famous Battle of New Market for the *Rockingham Daily Record*; her piece appeared in the May 2, 1913, issue. Her home was near the battlefield and had been in the direct line of fire. While her husband was out in the field treating the wounded, Lucinda stayed in her home with their four children. During the battle, the house was entered by both Union and Confederate troops. Lucinda recalled asking a Union captain not to enter a certain room so as not to frighten the children. He proceeded to grab her by the hair and, in Lucinda's words, "shoved me back. It was so dark, for I had quilts hung over the windows. The poor children were screaming and clinging to my dress." Thus we learn from recorded history another use

for quilts—to block out the sights and sounds of battle, as well as perhaps to offer some protection from stray bullets.

Lucinda was confined to a wheelchair for the last twenty-two years of her life. She spent much of her time doing needlework. One of her creations is this crazy patchwork piece in the shape of a large fish. The body of the fish is covered in small, 7/8" squares of fabric meant to resemble scales. A large appliquéd shell design represents the head of the fish, and a twisted floss fringe forms the mouth. Featherstitches, appliquéd stars, and silk tassels embellish the surface and edges of the piece.

It is said that for years the fish was draped over the top of the family piano. Eventually, Lucinda basted her little doll quilt to the back of the fish so that her first quilt would not be lost.

Accompanying the donation of the crazy patchwork fish and the doll quilt were two of Lucinda's other creations: a crazy quilt dated 1886 and a crazy quilt top, c. 1880.

Gift of Sylvia S. Moore

McCLEW/SPEIR WHITE WORK QUILTS
c. 1844 88" x 77" and 90" x 90"

Marion McClew Speir and her sister-in-law Mary McClew were both newlyweds when they decided to work together and make their white work quilts. Finished in 1844, the quilts were made in upper New York State, in the Fort Plains area. It is not known which quilt was made by which quilter.

A white work or whole cloth quilt is distinguished from other types of quilts in that its design comes from the quilting pattern used. Both of these quilts feature feathered leaves, flowers with round centers, and scallop motifs, but their different arrangements yield two unique designs. Extensive stipple quilting and cross-hatching cause the

designs on both quilts to appear in relief.

Mrs. Gray, the donor, found the quilts' history written in her mother's hand on a small piece of paper tucked inside an old flow-blue teapot. It is interesting to note that Mrs. Gray's father was a direct descen-dent of William Bradford, a Pilgrim and the first governor of the Plymouth Colony. Her great-grandmother was the quilt maker Marion McClew Speir.

Gift of Mrs. Basil Gray

THE BARLEY MEDALLION QUILT
c. 1847 101" x 102"

The Barley Medallion Quilt was made by Margaret Barnhart Barley (1821–1884) in Winchester, Virginia, for her daughter Katie's hope chest. A copy of a sketch of Katie made by a Civil War soldier accompanied the quilt when it was donated to the museum.

The quilt is constructed in a medallion style: A muslin center is appliquéd with flowers and a basket cut from another piece of fabric. The borders alternate between sawtooth pieced designs in pink and blue print fabrics and plain white strips. The outer sawtooth border is a pink-and-brown print. The fine hand quilting consists of vines of flowers, diagonal lines, and cross-hatching. Some of the quilting lines are only an eighth of an inch apart.

The edge of the quilt was formed by turning the top to the back.

Gift of Gordan C. Whitacre

HARRISON FAMILY ALBUM TOP

c. 1847—48   92" x 90"

This Baltimore Album quilt top was made for Bishop Keenor of the Baltimore Conference of the Methodist Episcopal Church, South. His niece Anna Hardesty Hank inherited the top. She married Charles D. Harrison, a descendent of the founder of the city of Harrisonburg, where the museum is located. The quilt was passed down to their daughter Miss Alice Harrison, who gave it to the donor, the granddaughter-in-law of Mr. and Mrs. Harrison.

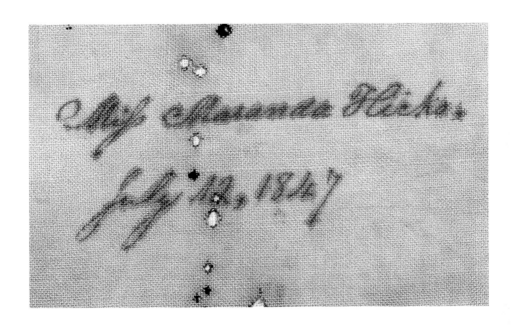

The quilt was never finished but was hemmed along the edges and used as a summer-weight bed covering. Consisting of twenty-five appliquéd blocks, it is accented with buttonhole, chain, and other assorted embroidery stitches using perle cotton and yarn. It serves as a wonderful learning piece in the collection.

The construction techniques used on the various blocks are interesting. The grapes on the lower left corner were appliquéd, then stuffed with batting through small holes opened in the weave of the fabric used as the backing. The cherries on the wreath near the center were stuffed by a different means: small slits were cut in the backing through which the cherries were stuffed, and the openings were then stitched closed. The roses in the urn on the center block of the bottom row were

appliquéd and stuffed from the front, while the four on the large wreath to the left of the center were quilted, stuffed from the back in sections, and then sewn closed.

Signatures and dates appear on the bottom row of the quilt. The open wreath block, second from the left, is inscribed "Miss Maranda Hicks / July 12, 1847," and the block at the lower right corner features an inked drawing of angels holding a scroll signed "Elizabeth Pearce, Jan. 1848." These were the only two ladies who signed and dated the blocks they created for the quilt top. Six other blocks are inscribed only with the following names: Samuel Price, Sen.; Martha Morton; Mary Pearce; Elizabeth G. Miles; Francis A. Commerell; Christina Commerell.

Gift of Mr. and Mrs. Charles M. Leigh

THE BRASHEARS BALTIMORE ALBUM QUILT
1848   95" x 97"

This quilt was made in memory of Joseph Brashears, a ship's captain from Mayo, Maryland, near Annapolis. He was lost in a shipwreck off the West Indies, and his friends and relatives had the quilt made as a memorial to him. In the center block is an inked inscription that reads, "Joseph Brashears / His quilt / Made by his friends / Presented to his cousin Ella Knighton / 1848." Over the years the quilt has been handed down in the family to those named Joseph or Josephine.

Made predominantly in shades of red and green typical of the era, the quilt features an interesting swag border and two blocks with figures on horseback. The horse and rider motifs were cut from another piece of fabric and appliquéd to the muslin background blocks. The donor's mother had told her that the figures represent George Washington.

Another interesting part of the quilt's construction is the small red cording that outlines each block.

Gift of Josephine Y. Barber

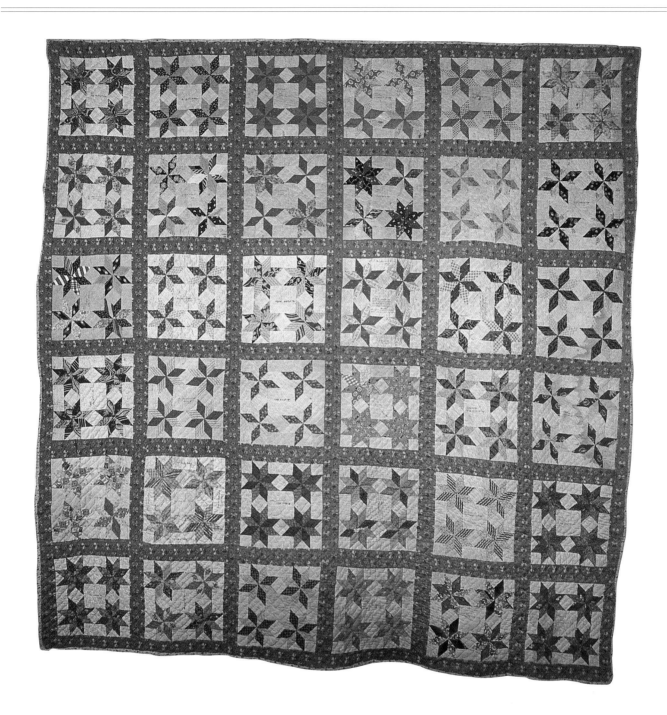

FOUR-STAR SIGNATURE/PRESENTATION QUILT
c. 1849–51   91" x 90"

After purchasing this quilt at an estate sale in Florida, the donor thought it should come back to Virginia, its state of origin. It was made by members of the High Bridge Presbyterian Church for their minister. The center block is inscribed, "To the Reverend S. D. Campbell / the Ladies of High Bridge / and hope he will accept this as a token of their regard. Farewell / Be of good comfort and the God of Love and Peace shall be with you. February 7, 1851 / Rockbridge Co., Virginia." Research has indicated that Reverend Campbell went on to serve churches in Georgia and Florida after leaving High Bridge.

The quilt consists of thirty-six blocks, each made up of four eight-pointed stars and bearing the signature of a church member. Some include dates. Constructed from cotton fabrics, the quilt is sashed with a tan floral print and is hand quilted overall with diagonal lines. It was documented in the Florida Quilt Heritage Project.

Gift of Julia Wernicke

SIX-POINTED STAR QUILT

c. 1850 92" x 72"

This quilt design is made up of six-pointed stars joined point to point with half-star blocks on the outer edges of the second and fourth rows. The center of each star appears to be constructed of six individual diamond-shaped pieces, but in fact each is made up of only three pieces. To save time, the double-diamond shapes at each star's center were cleverly cut by the quilt maker as one

piece rather than two. A line of quilting stitches down the middle of each gives the illusion of two distinct diamond pieces.

Three lines of echo quilting are found on each diamond, and triple-line cross-hatching covers the large diamonds that join the stars. The red and mustard-colored cotton fabrics that were used are typical of the period.

Although the red cloth appears to be printed with white dots, the dots are actually batting showing through holes left by the deterioration of the black dye used to print the design on the red fabric.

Gift of Geneva Funk McClung

TEXAS STAR QUILT

c. 1860 86" x 83"

Very little is known about this skill-fully made quilt, whose pattern is also known as the Star of Bethlehem. According to the donor, it was made by Louise Dinwiddie of Alexandria, Virginia. She and the donor's husband were cousins.

The quilt, for its age, is in excellent condition, and its color remains bright and clear. Dull red, yellow, and green printed fabrics are pieced on an off-white background, and a copper-toned madder print was used for the borders. A variety of quilting patterns, including rows of chevron stitches, double line scallops, stippling, and feather wreaths, was used. The narrow binding was made by turning the backing to the front of the quilt.

On a back corner of the Texas Star Quilt are inked letters that appear to be *LG*.

Gift of Nancy Gillis

HONEY BEE QUILT (VARIATION)
c. 1860 86 1/2" x 86 1/2"

A variation of the Honeybee pattern was used to construct this hand-pieced and hand-appliquéd quilt. Unlike the center of the traditional Honeybee block, which is a Nine Patch, this design has a one-piece, solid center. A like pattern is found in Barbara Brackman's book *Encyclopedia of Appliqué* and is dated c. 1840; it is untitled.

The setting consists of alternate plain blocks quilted with feather wreath motifs. Three borders frame the quilt, each featuring a different quilting pattern. A chevron design is on the first border, a double line chain is on the middle border, and a half circle design of concentric lines is quilted on the outer border.

Gift of Ann Ober and Mary Elliott in memory of Kathleen Davis Addison

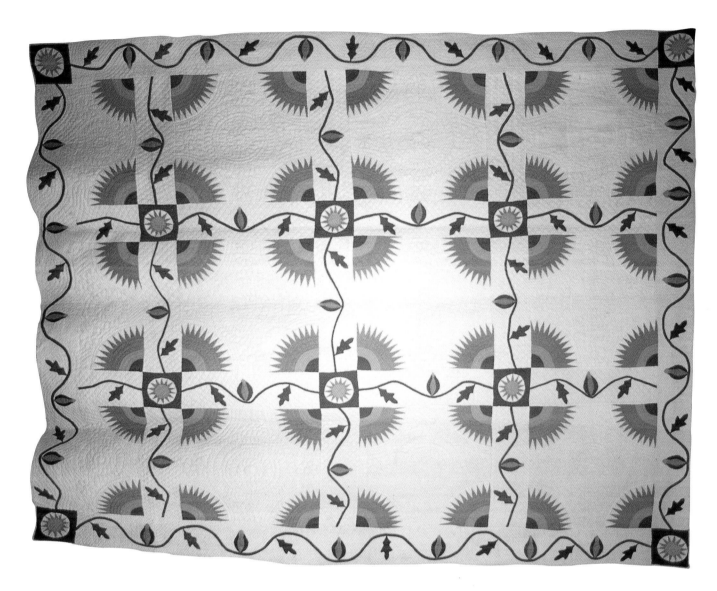

NEW YORK BEAUTY/ROCKY MOUNTAIN QUILT

c. 1865   82" x 100"

Also known as the Great Divide, this quilt was made in Highland County, Virginia, by Elizabeth Jane Davis Armstrong (1814–1915). It is constructed of nine full pieced blocks and three half blocks. The sashing is appliquéd in a vine, bud, and leaf design. Small corner blocks, each with a pieced sunflower pattern, are found at the intersections of the sashing strips. The quilting consists of cross-hatch-ing, echo and curved lines, sunflowers, and feather wreaths. Quilted in one corner of the piece are the initials *EDA*.

The New York Beauty/Rocky Mountain Quilt was featured on the cover of *Lady's Circle Patchwork Quilts* magazine in September 1994.

Gift of Diane Leonard Messick

DEMOCRAT ROSE/TEA ROSE QUILT (VARIATION)
c. 1870 88" x 88"

Mrs. Sam (Harriette) Moffett of Timberville, Virginia, made this exquisite appliquéd quilt. She lived from 1854 to 1949. For this piece, she used the popular fabrics of the day in red, pink, and green prints, as well as solid yellow.

With its layers of petal-edged shapes topped by a yellow circle, the design's center resembles that of the Democrat Rose pattern. The straight stems of the four smaller flower designs extending diagonally from the center toward the corners, however, more closely resemble the Tea Rose pattern,

as does the placement of the large green leaves at the center. Therefore, it appears that the pattern is a variation of one or more designs.

Very tiny, even stitches form the cross-hatch quilting design that covers the background. It is interesting to note that the block at the quilt's lower right corner is the only one with solid red in its four small flowers.

Gift of Mr. and Mrs. Beverly Bowers

TURKEY TRACKS QUILT TOP
1870   73" x 83"

Constructed of muslin and the rust-colored prints popular in the era, this top has an inked name and date in the lower right-hand corner: "Lydia Ann Humberston, Feb. 18, 1870." Pieced blocks are set with alternate plain blocks; a triple border frames the top.

Believed to have been made in the

Shenandoah Valley, this piece is especially appropriate for the Virginia Quilt Museum's collection—neighboring Rockingham County is known as the Turkey Capital of the World.

Gift of Dr. and Mrs. Thomas Keenan

EVENING STAR COMFORTER

c. 1880 79" x 65"

According to the quilt donor, Ella Wilson was in her teens when she made this quilt. She lived in Flintstone, Maryland. The pattern she chose is known by many names: Evening Star, Sawtooth Star, Ohio Star, and Optical Star. Pieced blocks of red, blue, green, and black fabrics on a white background are joined together by red-and-white-checked alternate blocks. It is said that Ella helped shear the sheep whose wool was used to make the batting. The quilt is neatly tied with green yarn.

Ella married into the McElfish family. The quilt was passed down to her son, who in turn gave it to the donor. No members of the McElfish family remain, so Ella's memory lives on through her quilt.

Gift of Mildred E. Lee

THE BAER CRAZY QUILT

c. 1880–92   61" x 79"

This crazy quilt was made over a period of years by the Baer sisters, who originally came from the Baer Lithia Springs area near Elkton, Virginia. Their family traces its roots to Adam Miller, the first settler of Rockingham County, Virginia. The four sisters—Virginia, Hattie, Emaline, and "Mit"—married and relocated to other areas and states, but they all gathered at Rehobeth Beach, Delaware, each summer to vacation. It is said that they and two sisters-in-law, Mary and Genie, sat on the front porch of the family home, with its view overlooking the ocean, and worked on the quilt.

When the top was completed in 1892, it

was given to the donor's mother and her
sister for safekeeping. They were the
favorite nieces of the Baer sisters, several of
whom never had children of their own.
When the donor married, in 1940, his aunt
lined the quilt top with heavy gray satin,
tied it with perle cotton, and presented it as
a wedding gift.

The quilt bears the popular embroidery
patterns of the day, including butterflies,
fans, and horseshoes. A charming little child
on snowshoes is pictured on a lithographed

ribbon near the center top of the quilt. Two
of the blocks, both dated 1884, are embroidered with the signature of former
Pennsylvania governor Robert E. Pattison.
One of the Baer sisters was the wife of a
prominent Methodist minister whose
church was in Pennsylvania; the governor
was most likely a member of the congregation.

Gift of Mr. and Mrs. William S. Brown

GREENE FAMILY ALBUM QUILT
1882   88" x 86"

Mary Ware Greene found this quilt in a trunk belonging to her late husband. The trunk had been stored in the attic for their entire married life, and she had never inquired as to its contents. Therefore, nothing is known about the quilt maker. It is believed that the quilt came down through her husband's family, who lived in Maryland. One block is signed "Cinnie C. Pearce / June 15, 1882."

The patterns for the blocks were appliquéd onto seventeen-inch squares.

Reverse appliqué was used in some areas. The designs are simplified versions of the elaborate Baltimore Album blocks. Of particular interest is the variety of quilting patterns used on the backgrounds; double line hearts, interlocking rings, flowers, leaves, clam shells, half and quarter feather wreaths, and cross-hatching are among them.

Gift of Mary Ware Greene

DIAMOND LOG CABIN CHILD'S QUILT
c. 1885 64" x 51"

Permelia Thayer Farley of New Ipswich, New Hampshire, made this quilt for the birth of her granddaughter Ruth Farley in 1885. The donor, Ruth Farley Massey of Winchester, Virginia, is the daughter of Ruth Farley and the great-granddaughter of the quilt maker.

The quilt is striking, with vivid shades of silk and other fine period fabrics in pink, yellow, purple, green, red, brown, and gray used in the strips, or "logs," surrounding the black center patches in each diamond block. The quilt maker's careful placement of the blocks has created bands of color running lengthwise down the quilt. A narrow border of dark-colored fabric frames the quilt.

Multicolored, twisted thread was used to embroider designs around the blocks and along the border's edges. Colorful thread ties made at the intersections of each block and at their centers were used to join the quilt top to the lining.

Parts of the original gray silk lining were still attached to the back of the quilt when it was given to the museum; they were in extremely fragile condition. A large fragment was preserved for study, and conservators covered the back of the quilt with new fabric to stabilize it.

Gift of Ruth Farley Massey

MOTHER'S BLESSING CRAZY QUILT
1885–86   66" x 53"

This exquisite crazy quilt was made by Marcia Tibbets Billings in Charles City, Iowa, for her son Martin's marriage to Cora Baltuff in May 1886. It is made of silks, velvets, and brocades embellished with lavish embroidery. The squares contain loving sentiments and symbols conveying a mother's wishes for a happy marriage and some subtle messages for the new bride. Floral blocks represent each of the seasons. On one block, an easel holds a painting of a cottage on a hill; on another, the "purse of thrift" reminds the bride to spend money wisely. A small "broom of neatness" on another block encourages her to keep the home tidy.

As indicated by the embroidered date, Mrs. Billings worked on the quilt from 1885–86. It is backed with brown silk and

tied, not quilted. Braided silk cording binds the edges of the quilt.

An embroidered open book in the upper left corner reads, "Mother's blessing goes with this quilt to her dear boy and his bride. Love lightened the labor of making and many earnest wishes for your future welfare, prosperity, and happiness were wrought in with the stitches."

The quilt was passed down to Martin's son Martin Hewett Billings, who in turn passed it on to his son (and the quilt maker's great-grandson) Martin Hewett Billings, Jr. Martin Jr. and his wife, who donated the quilt to the museum, live in Virginia.

Gift of Mrs. Lonnah Billings

CRAZY PATCH QUILT STRIPS
1886, 1887   61" x 13" each

W orked on a backing of tan glazed cotton, these elaborately embroidered strips were, according to family lore, made by the "admiring lady friends of Augustine Wills Neale." Each of the four strips consists of five thirteen-inch-square crazy quilt blocks. Constructed of velvets, silks, brocades, satins, and taffeta, the blocks are profusely embroidered with an array of decorative stitches and motifs popular at the time.

It is not known why the strips were never joined and the quilt completed. They were donated in 1991 by Mr. Neale's grandson. Handwritten notes accompanying the pieces state that Mr. Neale served in the

Army of the Confederacy and fought in the Battle of Cedar Creek. After the war, he continued his education, graduating in 1868 from Georgetown University. A native of Charles County, Maryland, Mr. Neale married, fathered eight children, and lived until 1932, when he died at the age of ninety-three.

It appears that each of his admiring lady friends was trying to outdo the other in her needlework. Museum visitors often wonder if one of the blocks was sewn by the lady who became Mrs. Neale. Perhaps she did not make a block, and that is why the quilt was never finished.

Gift of Mr. and Mrs. J. Matthews Neale, Sr.

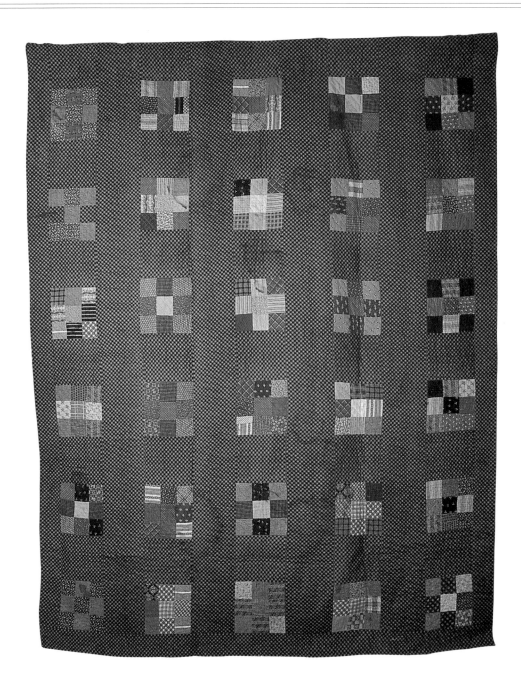

NINE-PATCH QUILT
c. 1889   92" x 73"

Constructed of thirty pieced blocks made of various brown and plaid polished cotton fabrics, this quilt is thought to have been made by an aunt of Mr. Russell Whitesell's of Tom's Brook, Virginia. The piece still retains some of its original glaze. The lining, or backing, of the quilt appears to be a vegetable-dyed (perhaps walnut-dyed) muslin. Brown thread was used to quilt the piece in diagonal and horizontal lines, with sixteen stitches to the inch. The date, 1889, is embroidered in chain stitching on the lower right corner of the back of the quilt.

The Nine-Patch Quilt is a good example of a Shenandoah Valley quilt made for utilitarian purposes.

Gift of Dr. and Mrs. Thomas P. Keenan

CHERRY WREATH QUILT

c. 1890 82" x 81"

This quilt was made by Laura Virginia Gruver of Reliance, Virginia. Born in 1872, Laura was the donor's mother. She made her appliquéd quilt prior to her 1895 marriage to Benjamin J. Hillidge.

The open-ended wreath design is believed to be an original. Solid green leaves are attached to the stemlike wreath, and stuffed solid-pink fabric cherries in groups of three are scattered between them. Several of the cherries are made of red fabric to indicate ripeness. Fine hand quilting adorns the piece with straight lines on the appliquéd blocks, double cross-hatching on the horizontal sashing, and feather swags with straight lines on the vertical sashing.

The donor attended the quilt museum's opening, in 1995, to see her mother's quilt on display. She was ninety-three at the time. Her quilt was the first given to the museum's collection.

Gift of Ruth H. Cone

THE CUNNINGHAM CRAZY QUILT TOP

c. 1890   42" x 72"

This quilt was made by Mae Moulton Stover Cunningham, a native of Lynchburg, Virginia. Mae's father owned a shoe factory in Lynchburg, but for some unknown reason, she was raised by her great aunts in Georgetown. She was sent to a Catholic school near Baltimore, were she excelled in her studies and won

many awards. Mae was an exceptional art student, and her talent is evident in the painted floral designs on her quilt. She was even known to have written a novel.

Her quilt top consists of twenty-eight blocks typical of the Victorian period. Each measures ten and a half inches square. The blocks feature flowers, animals, spiders, webs, fans, the initial *H*, and beautiful three-dimensional silk ribbon roses. The top remains unfinished.

Mae married William Newton Cunningham, and they settled near Marshall, Virginia, in a house that had been in the Cunningham family since the 1700s. Their son John inherited the quilt and gave it to the donor.

Gift of Carter Houck

LOG CABIN SILK QUILT
c. 1890   60" x 60"

Constructed in the "barn raising" Log Cabin pattern, this quilt is made of vibrantly colored silk strips. It was made in the Midwest; the quilt maker is unknown.

Four Log Cabin blocks form a white medallion center with an overlaid black velvet square. The small center squares of the other blocks in the quilt are also made of black velvet. The three blocks forming each corner have their centers embroidered with a starlike flower sewn with off-white perle cotton satin stitches.

An interesting striped silk fabric forms the four-inch-wide border of this quilt. The backing is a silk with wide brown and blue stripes. A tan-colored applied binding finishes the edges. The quilting consists of a diamond pattern done by hand in tan and black thread.

Over the years, some repairs have been made to the surface of the quilt with a sewing machine.

Gift of Dorothy Jarmoska

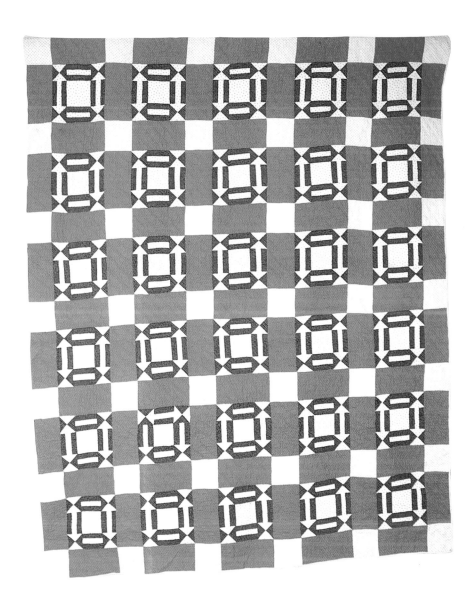

ARROW QUILT
1890   96" x 80"

This quilt was made by Martha Ellen Linaberg Clouser, who was born in Mountain Falls, Virginia, in 1862. She and her husband, John Quinton Clouser, had eleven children. The quilt was made for one of their daughters, Clara Mertyn Clouser Kline. Clara in turn passed it on to her son John Thomas Kline.

The quilt consists of thirty pieced squares made of printed cotton fabrics in pink and blue plaids. It is hand quilted with diagonal lines. In one corner of the back of the quilt is the inked inscription, "John Thomas / pieced by his / Grandmother Clouser / For Your Mother / 1890."

On one block, there is a mistake in the piecing of the Arrow pattern. Was this an oversight or an intentional error by the quilt maker? Perhaps she abided by the old quilter's adage, "only God can make the perfect creation."

The Arrow pattern is also known as Rope and Anchor or Fireside Visitor.

Gift of Pauline Liggett

RED-AND-GREEN ALBUM TOP

c. 1894 92" x 92"

The maker of this beautifully stitched quilt top is not known. Most of the red and green, seventeen-inch-square blocks are appliquéd using the onlaid method, in which the various shapes are cut from fabric, their raw edges turned under, and the pieces stitched onto a background square. A few of the blocks feature reverse appliqué—the design is cut from the top layer of fabric to reveal a contrasting fabric underneath. This technique is also known as inlaid appliqué.

The letters *SB* are appliquéd on one of the blocks in a leaf, vine, and cherry motif. Could these be the initials of the quilt maker?

The Red-and-Green Album Top is sashed with 1 1/2" strips of solid-red fabric.

Gift of J. Matthews Neale, Sr.

46

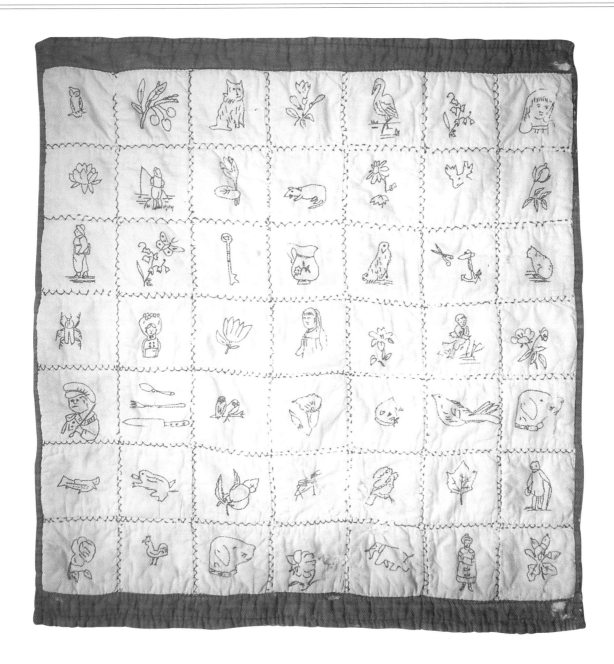

RED WORK DOLL QUILT
c. 1900   28" x 30"

Purchased at a yard sale in Greensburg, Pennsylvania, by the donor, this quilt features forty-nine charming little red work embroidered blocks, each measuring approximately 3 3/4" square. They depict children, animals, flowers, bugs, and household tools. The piece is machine quilted in 1/8"-wide rows down each side of the seam lines. Hand-embroidered chevron stitches were sewn over the area between the rows of stitching, producing an embroidered sashing between blocks. The top and the bottom of the quilt are bordered by a 1 3/4"-wide strip of Turkey red fabric. The two sides are bound with 3/8"-wide strips of the same red fabric.

When donated, the quilt was accompanied by a doll cradle, c. 1930, with a ticking mattress and a composition 1900 "sleepy eye" doll dressed in a hand-stitched gown.

Gift of Mrs. Sarah Watkins

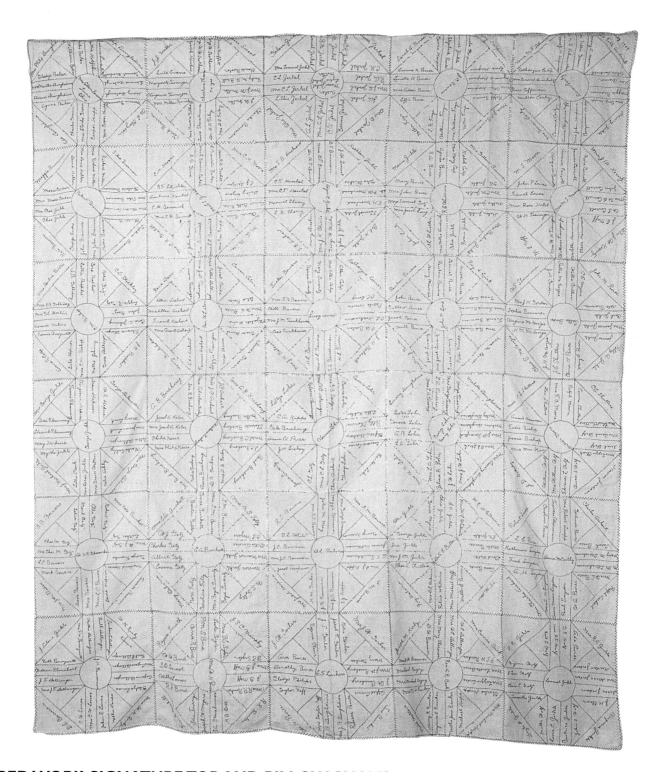

RED WORK SIGNATURE TOP AND PILLOW SHAMS
1909   78" x 70" and 31" x 30" each

These red work pieces belonged to Carrie R. Bird of Roselawn, Virginia. Their maker is unknown. Oral tradition tells us that the quilt top was made as a fund-raiser for a church. The names of church members are embroidered in red thread on a white background. (Makers of this type of quilt top customarily charged

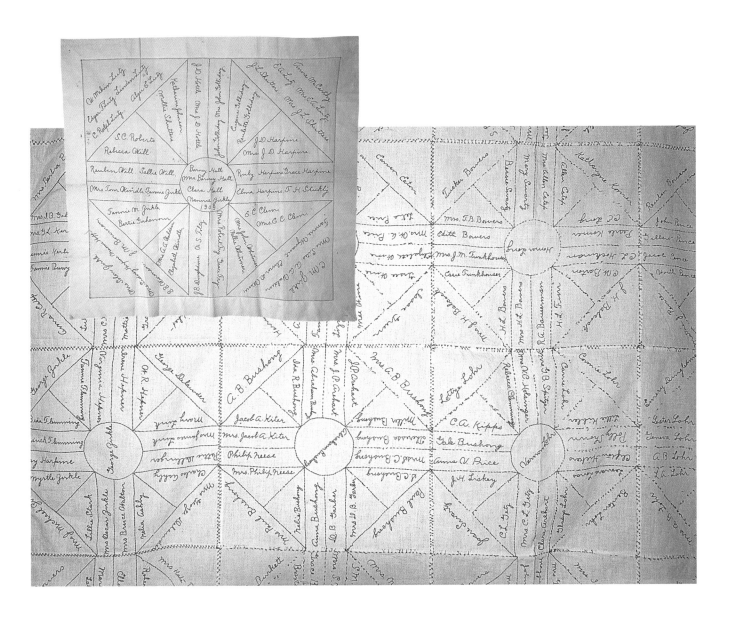

one sum, such as 25¢, to sew a name in the center of a block and another sum, such as 10¢, to place it around the sides of the block.) Featherstitching outlines each of the squares.

The companion pillow shams are each made of a single layer of fabric; decorative hem stitching frames a double-fabric border. Family names and the date 1909 are embroidered on the shams.

The quilt top was hemmed and used as a summer-weight covering, as evidenced by some fading and worn threads. The pillow shams appear to have never been used and remain in excellent condition.

Gift of Mr. and Mrs. J. Matthews Neale, Sr.

TOBACCO PREMIUMS QUILT TOP

c. 1914   81" x 76"

From about 1910 to 1915, tobacco companies included silk and flannel premiums in their packages that depicted such things as butterflies, flowers, famous people, and flags. This quilt top was made by Eula Adams Bartee, from the community of Mount Herman in the tobacco-growing area of Danville, Virginia. Eula saved the premiums from her husband's cigarette packages to make her quilt.

The flannel flags are of two sizes: five by eight inches, in the rows down each side of the quilt, and seven by ten inches, in the center section. They represent countries that existed in the early 1900s; the names of some (Siam, Persia) have since changed. The

flags were stitched together by machine.

When the quilt top was donated to the museum, it was accompanied by a pillow with four-by-two-inch silk premiums resembling tiny oriental carpets sewn in a circular design around a three-by-five-inch center premium.

Gift of Eleanor B. Allen

TEA ROSE QUILT (VARIATION)
c. 1920 68" x 81"

The donor of this quilt remembers her mother, Leona Branum Blosser, carefully taking it from storage in a blanket chest to show visiting lady friends. They marveled at its fine workmanship and were even more surprised when they learned that the quilt was made by a young man who lived in Rockingham County. Sadly, over the years his name has been forgotten, though the donor thinks it could have been Flory. It is said that he was a relative or friend of one of her mother's beaus. Leona married in 1924, so the quilt was made prior to that time.

The quilt is constructed of six large blocks, each measuring approximately 26 1/2" x 27". Solid fabrics in greens, red, yellow, pink, and orange were used. The four stems radiating diagonally from the center and the large green leaves in the middle are exactly like those on the Tea Rose pattern. However, the layered flower at the center resembles that of the Democrat Rose pattern. The four smaller flowers, though layered like the center flower, resemble neither pattern. A scalloped swag design, with whimsical lollipop motifs spaced along it, forms a border down the two long sides of the quilt. Quilted scallop designs fill the background of the blocks, and echo quilting with feathers adorns the borders.

Gift of Mrs. Julia Grandle

WAGON WHEEL QUILT
c. 1930   81" x 63"

This quilt was made by Sarah Jane Byler of Collinwood, Tennessee, in the 1930s. Rows of eight and nine pieced circular shapes alternate. Six different pieces of wedge-shaped fabric, all bright pastel prints typical of the 1930s, make up each wheel.

The background of the blocks and the backing of the quilt are made of feed sacks, as indicated by some inking that still remains on the lining. A label on the back of the quilt states that the batting was hand carded by the quilter. In the community in which the quilt was made, the quilting design used is known as the Shell design.

The quilt was inherited by Sarah's daughter, the donor, a Virginia resident.

Gift of Jane Byler Walrond

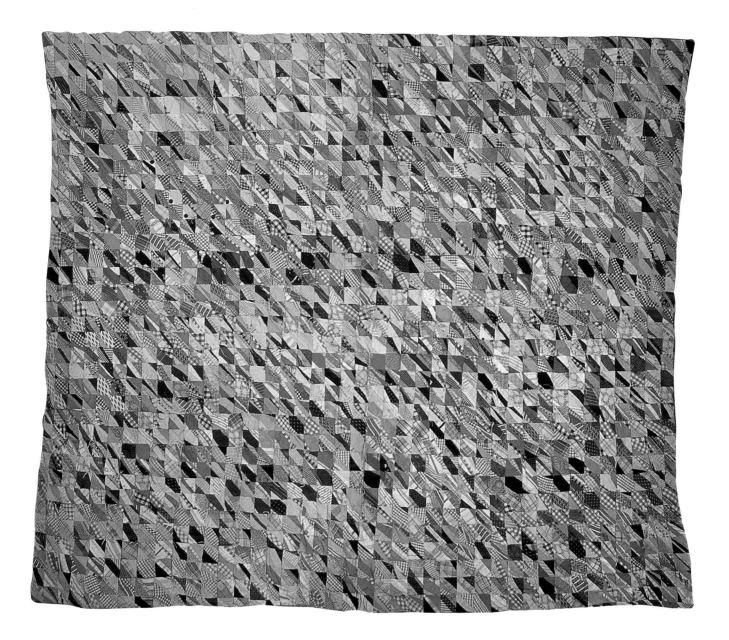

DEPRESSION-ERA STRING COMFORTER
c. 1930   76" x 65"

Elizabeth Meyerhoeffer of Rockingham County, Virginia, made this comforter—or "comfort," as it is often called in the Shenandoah Valley. Made from fabric scraps on hand, it is a genuine example of "making do" during the Great Depression.

Elizabeth constructed the comforter by stitching small strips of cloth onto fabric foundation squares. Each of the finished blocks measures two inches square, and some have as many as eight to eleven narrow pieces of material sewn onto them. A variety of fabrics were used, including cotton, fancies, and decorator fabrics in an array of colors. A repetition of black fabric unifies the design.

The piece has a thick cotton batting and is tied with assorted colors of thread.

Gift of Janet B. Downs

55

ONWARD AND UPWARD BIBLE CLASS QUILT
c. 1931–35   78" x 76"

A label on the lining tells us that this quilt was made by members of the Onward and Upward Bible Class of Kernstown Methodist Episcopal Church between 1931 and 1935. It is a signature quilt made in the Dresden Plate pattern. The piece has thirty-five blue-and-pink plates, each with twenty pointed spokes. The name of an adult of the congregation is embroi-

dered in script on each spoke. Pink floss was used on the blue fabric and blue floss on the pink.

The plates were appliquéd to the white background fabric, and the white circles at the center of each plate are embroidered with one to four names. One block is the cradle roll with the names of the babies born to members while the quilt was being

made. The quilting consists of outline stitching around the plates and in the spokes; a medallion design is quilted between the plates.

When the Kernstown church no longer had a pastor and was faced with closing, its members gave the quilt to nearby Stephens City Methodist Church. Later, a new minister was found. Both churches are still in operation today, and in 1995 they donated the quilt to the museum together.

Gift of Kernstown United Methodist Church and Stephens City United Methodist Church

GRANDMOTHER'S FLOWER GARDEN TOP
1940   92" x 77"

Mrs. Neves Robinson made this quilt top when she was living in New Jersey. She used a vivid, solid-purple fabric and printed fabrics popular at the time.

The flower garden is set in a star design. The English paper piecing technique was used to join the hexagons, and some still have the paper basted to their backs. Mrs. Robinson used black thread to sew the pieces together. She carefully turned the outer edges of the top under and basted them, but she never completed the quilt.

In 1997, while living in Blacksburg, Virginia, the maker sent the quilt top to the museum with a note stating that it was a donation "in memory of my son Ronald Robinson, who loved my quilting."

Gift of Neves Robinson

THE MARY SPITZER ETTER FAMILY

QUILTS AND QUILT TOPS

IN 1997, HARRISONBURG NATIVE MARY SPITZER ETTER donated her family's entire collection of quilts and tops to the Virginia Quilt Museum. The majority of the twenty-seven quilts were made by Mary's aunts, the five Spitzer sisters. Her father, Perry F. Spitzer, was the youngest child in the family of Emmanuel and Rebecca Andes Spitzer.

Only Hannah Spitzer (Brown), who moved to West Virginia after she married, left Rockingham County, Virginia. It is not known whether she and her twin, Jane Spitzer (Evers), did much quilting, but the other three sisters were prolific quilters. A single initial embroidered on the front of many of the quilts they made identifies the maker.

Sarah Josephine Spitzer (Walters) was born in 1847 and died in 1929. Known as Aunt Jose, she was widowed within a year of her marriage. A son, Eli Gunning Walters, was born after his father's death. Josephine especially liked making Log Cabin quilts, as well as other traditional designs.

Margaret Melinda Spitzer (Jones) was born in 1851 and died in 1934. She was called Aunt Mag by the family. In 1871 she married Jessie Jones, and they had two children. Aunt Mag was particularly fond of making crazy quilts and is remembered for her use of the brier stitch to embellish them. She also enjoyed making doll clothes for children and crocheting.

Ellen Rebecca Spitzer was born in 1853 and died in 1933. She excelled at all types of needlework. Her quilts display expert piecing and quilting in a wide variety of patterns. Aunt Ellen was known throughout the community as one who cared for the ill and helped with various events, such as weddings and receptions.

Aunt Ellen had one daughter: Irene Vernie Spitzer (1883–1927). Irene was called Cousin Vernie and made two of the tops and one of the quilts in the collection. They are colorful scrap quilts made in Four Patch, Sixteen Patch, and Single Patch designs.

Several quilts in the collection were made by relatives in New York and friends in Harrisonburg. The donor's mother, Mabel Spitzer, is responsible for having had many of the unfinished blocks and tops put together and either tied or quilted by her neighbors Berta and Effie Long. Therefore, some of the Spitzer sister quilts have blocks dating back to the late 1800s, but they are sashed and backed with fabric from the 1930s. The foresight shown in preserving these pieces, rather than storing them unfinished in the attic, is to be commended.

Mary Etter followed in her mother's ways by giving the collection to the museum. She also donated numerous other items, including handmade pieces of clothing, lace, needlework tools, and pattern books, all attesting to the sewing skills of the Spitzer sisters. As the last member of her family, she "wanted things to go on in memory of my people" and entrust the quilts to a place where they would be cared for and displayed for all to enjoy. We thank her for sharing them with us and for preserving her family's quilting heritage.

Donor of the quilts made by her aunts the Spitzer sisters, Mary taught school in the Shenandoah Valley for thirty-nine years. She has since had special costumes made, in the 1890s style, to wear when she visits area schools and when she speaks about her family's history at various events. A 1934 graduate of Harrisonburg State Teachers College, now James Madison University, Mary had one dress made in dark purple and another in a purple-and-gold print, the school colors. She is pictured here in one of the dresses, carrying a stylish parasol made to accompany it.

SAMPLER CRIB QUILT

c. 1880   39 1/2" x 44"

According to the donor, this little quilt may have been made for the birth of Ellen Spitzer's daughter, "Vernie," who was born in 1883. Hand pieced and quilted, the quilt is a sampler featuring such traditional designs as Wonder of the World,

Turkey Tracks, T Block, Caesar's Crown, and, in the center, a Star Medallion. Pieced borders were added around the variously sized blocks in order to make them all fit together.

Gift of Mary Spitzer Etter

PINEAPPLE LOG CABIN QUILT

c. 1875 80" x 90"

This quilt is constructed of cotton, wool, and some silks. It is hand quilted and, because of its pieced back, considered a double-sided quilt. A pink embroi- dered *J* on the upper corner identifies the maker as Sarah Josephine Spitzer (Aunt Jose).

Gift of Mary Spitzer Etter

YELLOW CENTER LOG CABIN QUILT

c. 1875   80" x 97"

Made of wool, cotton, and silk, this quilt was hand pieced and hand quilted by Sarah Josephine Spitzer. The embroidered *J* in the upper left corner identifies her as the maker. With a randomly pieced backing of scraps, the quilt is doubled-sided.

Gift of Mary Spitzer Etter

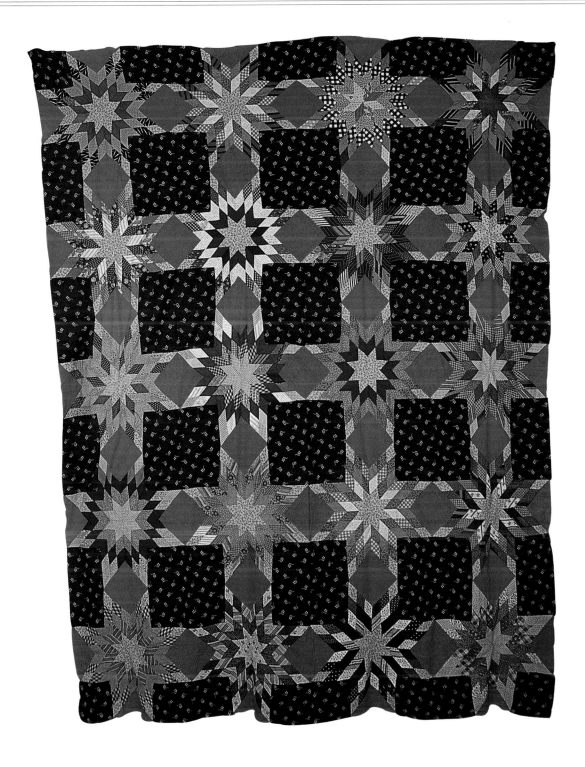

SHIP'S WHEEL TOP

c. 1875 72" x 90"

The *J* at the top of this variation of a Star pattern tells us that it was made by Sarah Josephine Spitzer. It is a cotton quilt top made of vibrantly colored scraps featuring many of the popular prints of the era.

Gift of Mary Spitzer Etter

ALBUM SQUARE QUILT
c. 1890 79" x 93"

This beautiful hand-pieced and hand-quilted design features many of the era's lovely fabrics in a popular Album pattern. The lavender-colored, embroidered initials *ES* in the corner tell us that the quilt was made by Ellen Spitzer.

Gift of Mary Spitzer Etter

DOUBLE X QUILT

72" x 90"

T his charming pattern is highlighted by the array of scrap fabrics used on a muslin background and by the exqui- site hand quilting, with eighteen stitches to the inch. It was made by Ellen Spitzer, and her embroidered, lavender *E* marks the quilt.

Gift of Mary Spitzer Etter

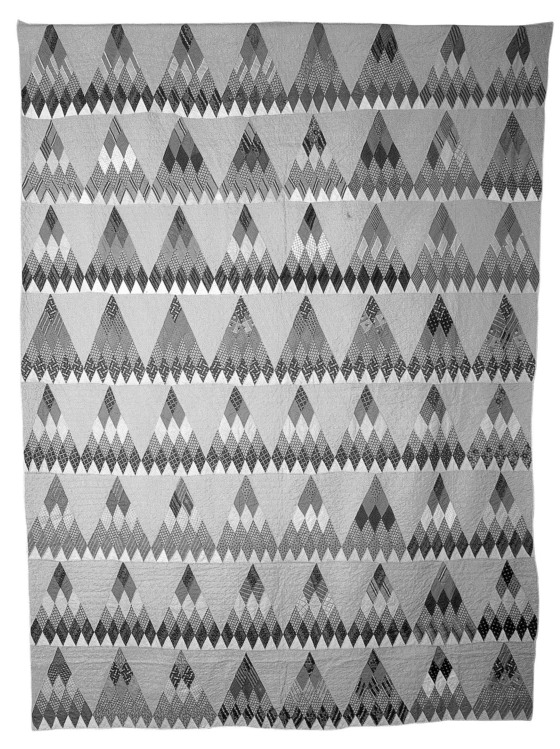

TEE PEE OR SUGARLOAF QUILT
c. 1890   70" x 92"

Made of muslin and cotton prints in soft shades of orange, gold, and brown, this quilt is hand pieced and hand quilted. The diamond-based design exemplifies the work of an accomplished "piecer." The quilt was made by Ellen Spitzer and is initialed on the back.

Gift of Mary Spitzer Etter

VARIABLE STAR QUILT
c. 1890 82" x 93"

This is a tied comfort whose star blocks are made of scraps and alternate with plain blocks of a green-and-yellow print fabric that was very popular at the time. The quilt is tied with bright gold-en perle cotton thread. A pink *J* embroidered at the top identifies the maker as Sarah Josephine Spitzer.

Gift of Mary Spitzer Etter

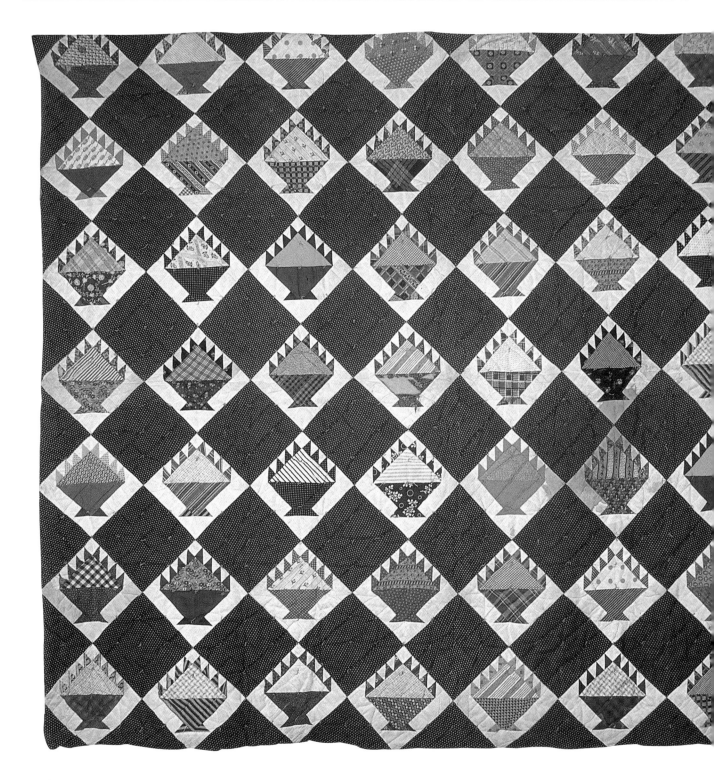

BASKET OF TRIANGLES QUILT

c. 1890   68" x 81"

This quilt's blocks were pieced by Ellen Spitzer; the letter *E* is embroidered on them. The donor's mother purchased the lovely paisley backing and employed the Long sisters of Harrisonburg to complete the quilt.

Gift of Mary Spitzer Etter

The Spitzer sisters with their parents. Back row (left to right): Ellen, Margaret, Sarah Josephine, Jane, and Hannah. Front row: Emmanuel and Rebecca Andes Spitzer.

FEATHERED STAR QUILTS
1880, quilted 1930s   80" x 100" and 83" x 102"

The blocks for these two quilts were made by Ellen Spitzer. After her death, the donor's mother, Mabel Spitzer, had them sashed together and quilted by her neighbors Berta and Effie Long.

The fabric used indicates that the quilting was done in the 1930s.

Gift of Mary Spitzer Etter

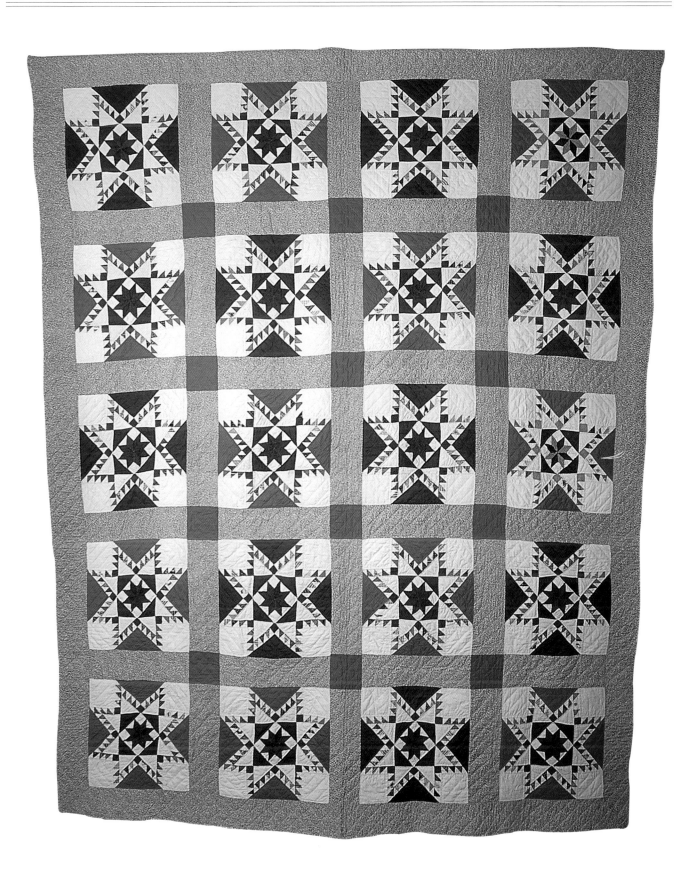

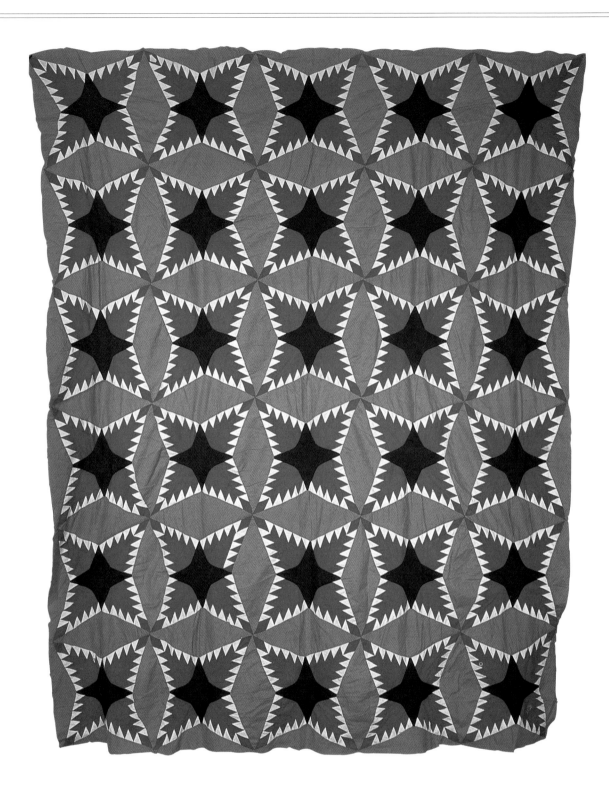

PINE BURR TOP

c. 1890 71" x 82"

This is a cotton top pieced by Ellen Spitzer, as indicated by her initial. The quilt was never finished. Nonetheless, its small, feathered triangles and bold color scheme make for an interesting and intricate piece.

Gift of Mary Spitzer Etter

CARPENTER'S SQUARE TOP

c. 1890   83" x 94"

This cotton top was pieced by Ellen Spitzer, who sewed her initial in the corner. It was never finished, probably because it became so out of shape due to the stretching of the bias-cut fabric pieces. It is an interesting pattern and a complicated one to construct.

Gift of Mary Spitzer Etter

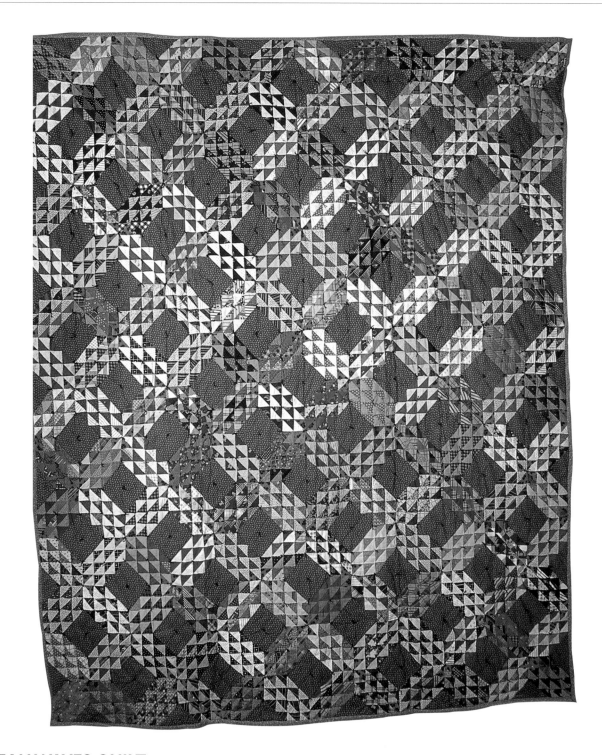

OCEAN WAVES QUILT
c. 1900   78" x 85"

This tied comfort was probably pieced by Ellen Spitzer. Not only did Ellen make more than twice as many quilts as her sisters, but she alone repeated fabrics in her pieces. The Ocean Waves Quilt contains many of the fabrics used in her other creations.

Made of cotton, it is like an encyclopedia of the fabrics of the era.

Gift of Mary Spitzer Etter

FLYING GEESE QUILT
c. 1900   83" x 87"

Which Spitzer sister made this quilt is unknown. It is constructed of strips of varying numbers of "geese" triangles and is sashed with plain strips of pink, printed fabric. The fabrics are typical of the era.

The piece is machine quilted with straight lines and cross-hatching.

Gift of Mary Spitzer Etter

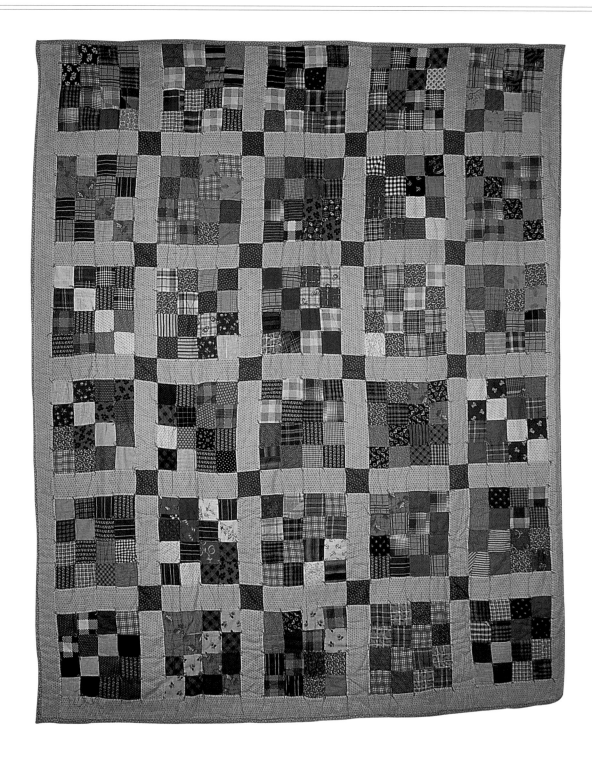

SIXTEEN-PATCH QUILT

c. 1900   69" x 84"

The blocks in this quilt are believed to have been pieced from scraps by Ellen Spitzer's daughter, Irene Vernie Spitzer. Later, the blocks were sashed together and the quilt tied by the Long sisters of Harrisonburg at the request of the donor's mother.

Gift of Mary Spitzer Etter

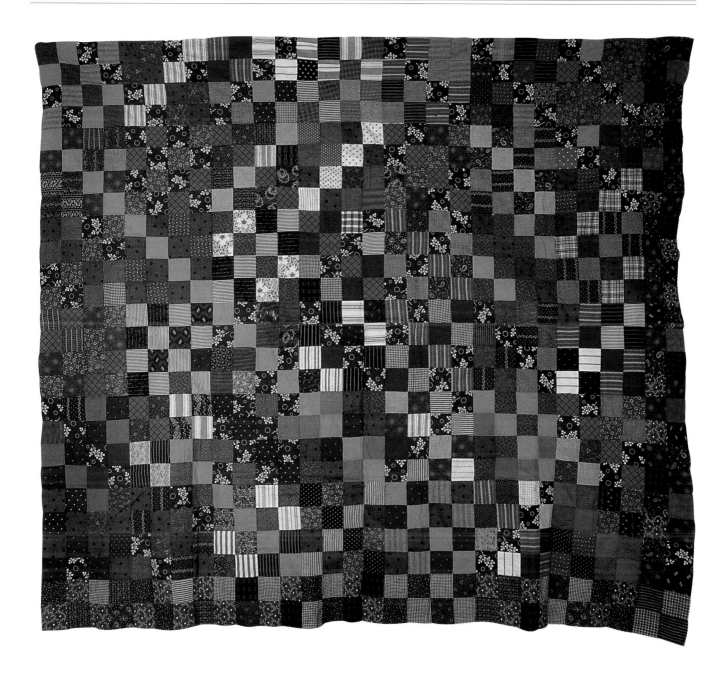

SCRAP FOUR-PATCH QUILT
blocks c. 1900   68" x 90"

The top of this quilt was made by Cousin Vernie (Irene Vernie Spitzer), and the donor's mother had it backed and tied by her neighbors the Long sisters. A lovely black, purple, and green printed fabric was chosen for the back; supposedly, it was purchased from either the Joseph Neys store or a small fabric store called Fitzer's. Both businesses were once part of Harrisonburg's downtown shopping scene and no longer exist.

Gift of Mary Spitzer Etter

COTTON CRAZY TOP
c. 1900   70 1/2" x 80"

Margaret Spitzer Jones (Aunt Mag) made this colorful crazy quilt out of cotton scraps. It is embellished with her favorite decorative embroidery: the brier stitch. Margaret used small leftover quilt blocks to form the centers of several of her crazy squares.

Gift of Mary Spitzer Etter

BACHELOR'S PUZZLE QUILT (VARIATION)

c. 1900   84" x 96"

This quilt is believed to have been made by relatives of Emma Mabel Baldwin Spitzer, the donor's mother. Her family lived in New York State. The donor remembers that the quilt was always on her mother's bed.

Note the interesting Streak of Lightning, or zigzag, pattern on the borders.

Gift of Mary Spitzer Etter

DRESDEN PLATE QUILT
67" x 84"

Berta and Effie Long of Harrisonburg made this quilt for Mary Spitzer and another one like it for her sister Ruth Spitzer. They were birthday gifts commissioned by the girls' mother, Mabel Spitzer, who gathered fabric scraps from old family dresses, aprons, and pajamas to give to the Long sisters for use in the quilts.

Gift of Mary Spitzer Etter

GREEK SQUARE QUILT
69" x 88"

This quilt was made as a wedding gift for Mary Spitzer Etter by her cousin Clara Reynolds and her daughter Phyllis Lindsey. They lived in Stephen- town, New York, when the tied comfort was made.

Gift of Mary Spitzer Etter

THE LUCY CATHERINE BOWIE QUILTS

THE LUCY CATHERINE BOWIE PORTION OF THE MUSEUM collection consists of thirteen quilts and tops. Some of the pieces were made solely by Lucy Catherine, some were made by members of her family with her assistance, and some were acquired by Miss Bowie for study purposes.

After her death in 1997, the quilts were inherited by a cousin, Sarah Shaffer, who left them in the care of the museum until an exhibit honoring Lucy Catherine could be mounted. During the summer of 1998 the quilts were displayed in the Beyer and Bowie exhibition, which also featured the work of another Virginia quilter, Jinny Beyer. Ms. Shaffer then decided to keep one of the quilts and offer the others for sale. Contributions that might enable the museum to purchase the quilts were sought, and within two weeks, quilt guilds, clubs, and individuals from across the state and the country had made the donations necessary to keep the quilts permanently in Virginia. Lucy Catherine would have been honored to know that so many hold her work in such high regard.

Born in Culpeper, Virginia, on June 10, 1914, Lucy Catherine Bowie left a legacy of quilts and writings on quilt making. A graduate of Averett College, she was one of the first women to do graduate work at the University of Virginia. She taught school for eight years before entering the printing business with her brother. They established the *Rappahannock News* in 1949. Of eighteen months spent learning to be a linotype operator, at the time considered to be a man's job, she remarked, "there's nothing like the sharp perfection in four hundred pounds of pressure." Later, she worked for the *Culpeper Star Exponent* and the *Orange Review*. In 1971, she became the editor of the *Eagle* newspaper.

Eight generations of Lucy Catherine's family, the Bowies and the Stringfellows, lived in Culpeper and Rappahannock County. The art of quilt making was passed from generation to generation, and her quilts were often the result of several family members' efforts. They all loved to quilt and always worked together. Lucy Catherine's aunt Lucy Ann Stringfellow, known as Aunt T, worked on many quilting projects with her and no doubt passed on many quilting tips. Fine quilting and lovely color combinations, using scraps on hand, produced winners at the Virginia State Fair year after year.

Lucy Catherine's quilts exemplify expert quilting techniques and countless hours of research and planning. She kept a written record of her thoughts on each quilt, her research pertaining to specific patterns and themes, and sketches of her designs. Of her quilting, she said, "I'm satisfied with nothing but my very best, and I never get it . . . the mechanics of quilting is the same thing. There's a sense of satisfaction in working all evening to get one tiny square just right, by hand."

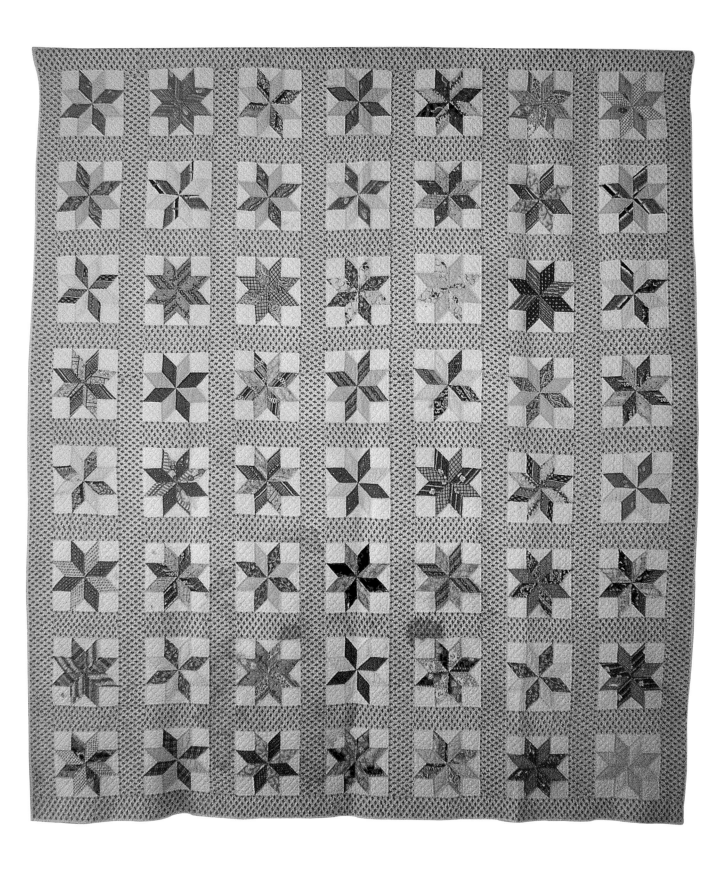

LEMOYNE STAR QUILT
blocks c. 1840, quilted 1946   88" x 92"

The top of this quilt was pieced by Lucy Catherine's maternal grandmother, Sarah Judson Broadus (1836–99), as a young child. It was a little girl's "learning piece"—meaning that Sarah was taught to sew by piecing the quilt blocks. Sarah married, raised a family, and kept the quilt top in a trunk. She told her children about making it.

In 1946, when the quilt top was over a century old, Sarah's daughter Lucy Ann Stringfellow said to her niece Lucy Catherine, "Let's quilt the old top"—and they did. It is now an early example of carefully executed quilt conservation techniques. In Lucy Catherine's words, "Dry rotted pieces were backed with cotton net and quilted down for strengthening." The quilting was meant to "hold the fragile pieces securely and not for show." The net repairs are visible on some parts of the quilt.

Also interesting is the fact that the top was pieced with homespun "thick and thin" thread. According to Lucy Catherine, thread spun on a big spinning wheel, rather than commercially made, was thick in some places and thin in others.

Gift of the Skyline Quilters' Guild

BLUE POINT STAR QUILT
1951   77" x 96"

Robert Eliza Stringfellow Bowie, Lucy Catherine's mother, made this quilt from scraps of family clothing. The material includes pieces from a dress worn on the first day of school, a costume used in a school play, and a blouse worn while on the debating team.

The blue fabric in the stars gives the impression of it being a blue quilt. The blue in the stars also gives the quilt its name and contrasts with two shades of white in the background blocks. The quilt has a batting made of hand-carded wool and is trimmed with handmade hairpin fringe.

Gift of the Virginia Consortium of Quilters

FLOWER GARDEN QUILT

1935–53   84" x 88"

This is the first quilt made by Lucy Catherine Bowie entirely on her own. Its colors are typical of those used in the 1930s, when it was begun. Miss Bowie started it during her first year of teaching, when she lived away from home. She said of the quilt, "It was worked on, put away, taken out, [and] put away many times before exasperation said finish it and be done!" The green fabric represents paths of grass in the garden. Red would have been used to symbolize brick walks. Lucy Catherine noted, "In Tidewater, I saw one put together with yellow; they used sand for paths."

Gift of the Madison County Quilters' Guild, Thelma Shirley (The Little Shop), and Charlotte Veregge

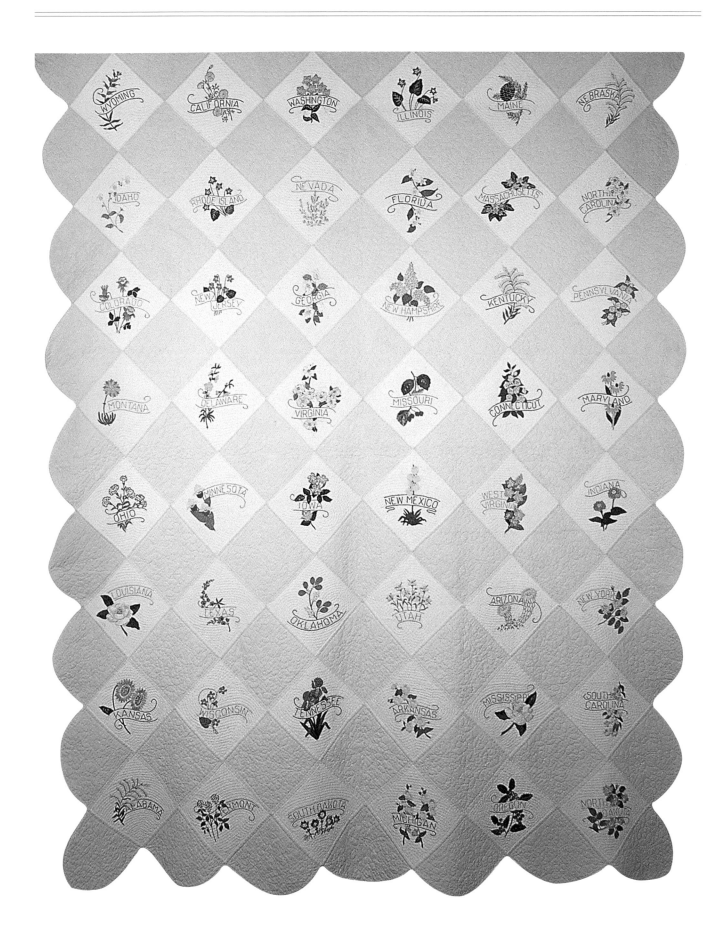

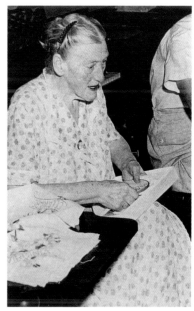

Lucy Ann Stringfellow embroidering a quilt block.

STATE FLOWERS QUILT
1956   82" x 102"

This quilt was embroidered by Lucy Ann Stringfellow (Aunt T) and quilted by her niece Lucy Catherine Bowie. The stamped flower block patterns did not stipulate colors, but at Miss Stringfellow's request, the Culpeper Library procured the loan of a hand-colored volume of American flowers from the Virginia State Library.

The blocks were sewn on cloth from cotton flour sacks. It was Lucy Catherine's job to purchase the softest sacks at the feed mill and hand dye those used for the alternate plain blocks. She said it took many attempts to mix the exact shade of pink desired by Aunt T.

Miss Stringfellow was eighty years old when she began the quilt. She worked on it for a year before her death on Easter Sunday 1956. Lucy Catherine finished the remaining six blocks, quilted the piece, and entered it as her aunt had wished in the Virginia State Fair that September. It was awarded Best Needlework of Show. "I never entered anything in the fair after that," said Lucy Catherine.

The viewer will note that the quilt does not have blocks for Hawaii or Alaska, which were not yet states.

Gift of the Virginia Consortium of Quilters

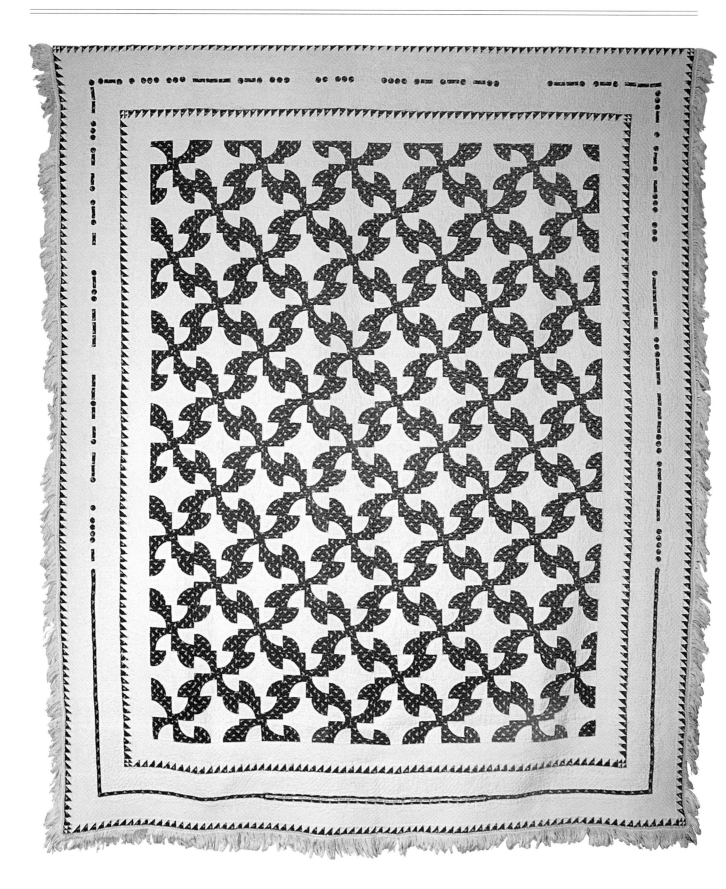

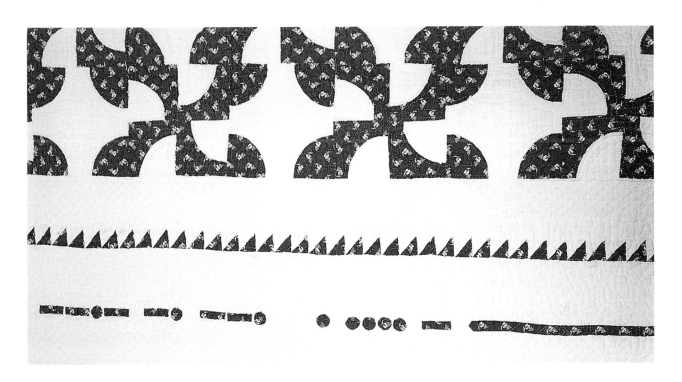

SOLOMON'S PUZZLE QUILT
1976   75" x 88"

This is Lucy Catherine Bowie's bicentennial quilt. She worked on it in her spare time for a period of two and a half years. She said she chose the purple-and-white color scheme to represent the verse "purple mountains' majesty above the fruited plain" in the song "America the Beautiful." The purple fabric was purchased and is an example of what was available in the 1970s; the dye was not colorfast when exposed to light for a period of time. Feed sacks were used for the white background.

The pattern is a version of the Drunkard's Path. Lucy Catherine said that her quilt had a dual meaning depending on whether one called it Solomon's Puzzle or Drunkard's Path. All the plants grown in America that can be used to produce spirits are depicted in the background quilting. The piece's borders are appliquéd with dots and dashes—Morse code representing a Biblical admonition from Proverbs 13:15. At the bottom of the quilt, the maker signed and dated her work in Morse code.

The Solomon's Puzzle Quilt is trimmed with handmade hairpin lace fringe. In 1977, it took Best in Show at the National Quilting Association's National Show, and it won Best Bicentennial in the 1981 NQA Show.

Gift of Anne Morgan, Louise Nichols, Dorothy Reid, Le Rowell, Ruth Thompson, the Cardinal Quilters' Guild, and the Shenandoah Valley Quilters' Guild

NECKTIE COVERLET

78" x 88"

It is thought that Lucy Catherine Bowie pieced this coverlet, but when is not known. The fans are made from men's old neckties and are a wonderful array of flamboyant prints and colors. The back-ground fabric is heavy taffeta.

The piece is not lined and has a neatly turned hem.

Gift of the Country School Quilters' Guild

FRAMED MEDALLION QUILT

c. 1840   88" x 99"

The maker of this quilt is unknown. It was purchased by Miss Bowie at an estate auction in the northern part of West Virginia in the 1940s. Lucy Catherine wrote that it is of museum quality and was "designed by a true artist and executed by a master craftsman." She added, "I wish I had known her." The quilt is made of a variety of printed fabric pieces, and its many pieced patterns always amaze visitors.

Gift of the Robert E. Lee Chapter, #60, Questers

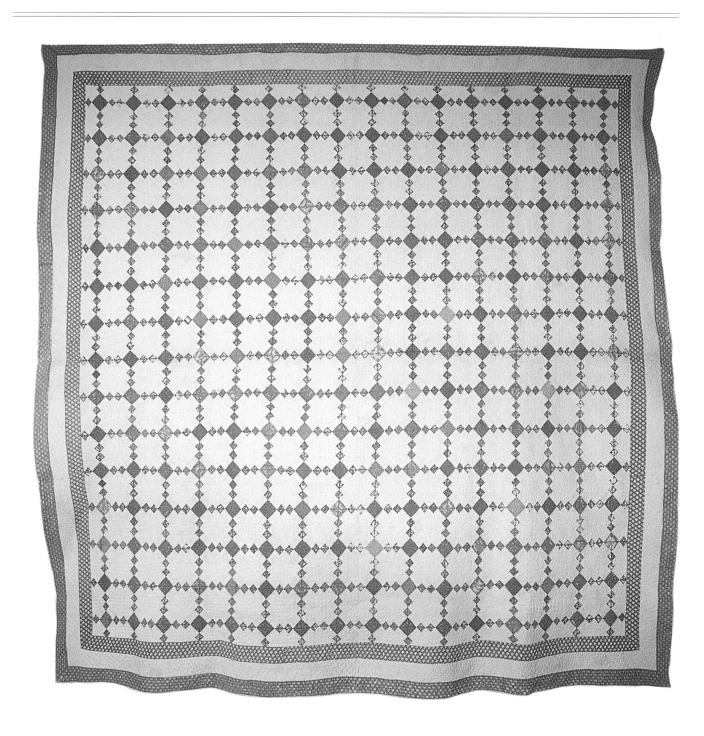

IRISH CHAIN (PUSS IN THE CORNER)
c. 1870   89" x 89"

One of Miss Bowie's study quilts, this was purchased at an auction in the 1940s. Lucy Catherine admired its fine craftsmanship. She identified it as an Irish Chain pattern, but further research has suggested that it is the Puss in the Corner design.

"Elizabeth, Chambersburg, Pa. No. 3" appears in ink on the quilt. The inscription suggests that Elizabeth had nine more quilts to make before her "useful dozen" was completed.

Gift of the Cabin Branch Quilters' Guild

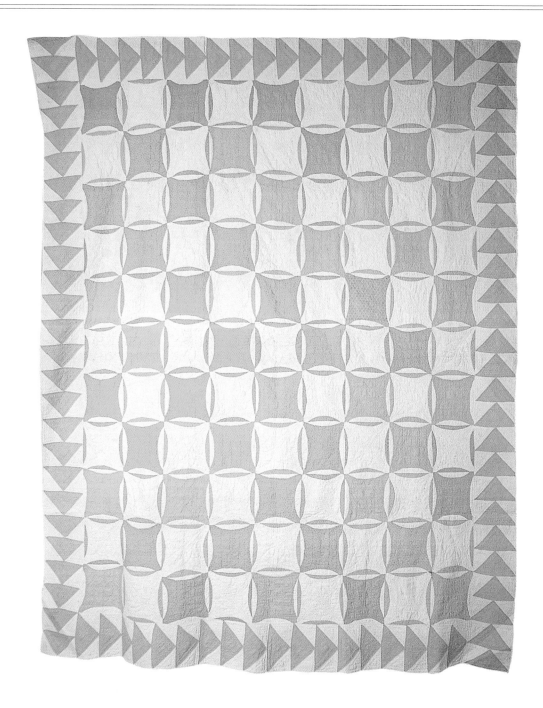

ORANGE PEEL (ROB PETER TO PAY PAUL) QUILT

c. 1880   79" x 98"

This quilt was purchased for study by Lucy Catherine Bowie. It was obtained at an auction of the Bushong family estate. Miss Bowie believed that the fabric was hand dyed due to the uneven coloring. She related how the pattern came to be named in her notes: "During LaFayette's 1825 visit to America, he was observed peeling an orange peel in the aristocratic French fashion. A lady was inspired to design this quilt pattern. When made in a color other than yellow or orange, it is called 'Rob Peter to Pay Paul,' which is any pattern of equal exchange in two squares."

Gift of Paula and Terry Golden

SILK PIECED TOP

c. 1889   39" x 67"

This quilt top, another of Miss Bowie's study pieces, was never completed, and its maker is unknown. The silk triangles are pieced on paper foundations that still remain on the back. The date January 2, 1889, is printed on one of the papers.

Gift of Judy Meyer in honor of her husband, Merle Meyer

TULIP QUILT (CROSS AND CROWN VARIATION)

c. 1900   74" x 96"

This quilt was one of Lucy Catherine Bowie's study quilts. She purchased it at an estate auction in the 1940s. She noted that the piece was well quilted and that the cloth appeared to be pre–World War I; the white fabric was perhaps homespun.

Interestingly, the blocks seem to be pieced, but careful examination reveals that they are Nine Patches with pieces appliquéd on top to produce the center cross motif and corner tulips. Feathered circles and plumes make up the quilting patterns.

Gift of Cathy Crocker and the Piecemakers Quilt Guild

TENTS OF ARMAGEDDON

c. 1900   74" x 83"

This pieced top is made of many scraps of fabric popular at the turn of the century. The maker and location of origin are unknown. It was used by Lucy Catherine Bowie as a study piece.

Gift of Cheri Clum in memory of Elizabeth Clum

VIRGINIA HERITAGE QUILT

c. 1986–88   96" x 87"

T his quilt was a group project of the
Virginia Consortium of Quilters, the
state quilt organization. It features
appliquéd scenes of various points of interest across the state of Virginia, such as the
Natural Bridge, Blanford Church, and the
Blue Ridge Mountains. Traditional pieced
blocks associated with the state, like "Virginia

Reel" and "Dolley Madison's Star," are set amongst the appliquéd squares. Along the sides of the quilt are blocks portraying each of the US presidents born in Virginia.

For ten years, the quilt was exhibited at quilt shows and events across the state. It was exhibited at the Virginia General Assembly's 1995 session before it was given to the quilt museum in August of that year.

Gift of the Virginia Consortium of Quilters

VIRGINIA QUILT MUSEUM (BELLE GROVE) ALBUM QUILT

1991   98" × 98"

This was the museum's first fund-raising raffle quilt. It was designed by
Anna Holland and quilted by Margie
Hockman. The blocks were appliquéd by
quilters from all across Virginia.

Made of printed and hand-dyed cotton

fabrics, the Baltimore Album–style blocks
feature Belle Grove Plantation in
Middletown, Virginia, where the museum
had its beginnings. A hand-drawn picture of
the house appears above the center basket
block. Belle Grove was built by Maj. Isaac

Hite, and three generations of Hite family names are inked on the quilt blocks. On the floral vine border are the inked names of the contemporary quilters who worked on the piece. All of the inked inscriptions were executed by Lesley Claire Greenberg.

The raffle raised more than twenty thousand dollars, money that was used to start the museum. The quilt was won by the Skyline Quilters' Guild, of the Front Royal/Strasburg area of Virginia. The guild thought that such an integral part of the museum's history belonged in its permanent collection, and when the museum opened in 1995, the quilt was returned.

Gift of Skyline Quilters' Guild

THE VIRGINIA QUILT

c. 1991   72" x 80"

The idea for this quilt originated at the first meeting of the 1989–90 Quilters Unlimited of Northern Virginia Executive Board. The board was looking for a group project that could involve all chapters and members, and making a Virginia quilt seemed to be the answer.

Fabric packets with instructions were distributed to all of the chapters. Any aspect of Virginia that was of interest to a member could be depicted on a block for the quilt. Some of the designs are original, and others are patterns handed down through the years. The blocks are both pieced and appliquéd using a variety of hand and machine techniques. Each measures six inches square.

The quilt celebrates the diversity of the state: its geography, its history, and its people. It is hand quilted.

Gift of Quilters Unlimited of Northern Virginia

TAJ REFLECTIONS QUILT
c. 1990–92   93" × 93 1/2"

This quilt is made up of forty-nine blocks, each measuring twelve inches square. Various piecing and appliqué techniques were used, and some of the blocks are embellished with embroidery. All of the piecing, appliqué, assembly, and quilting was done by hand. The quilt was a group project of the Waterford (Virginia) Quilters' Guild. It was made to be a raffle quilt, but the guild members could not part with it after its completion and kept it for display at their annual quilt show.

The pieced block design is an original by guild member Trudy Springer. It was inspired by the tile pattern on the main pavilion floor of the Taj Mahal in India. From her sketches of garden flowers, the bas-relief carvings in marble and inlaid work of the Taj Mahal, and her photographs of nature, Trudy also designed the floral patterns. The reflection or reverse image of almost every flower appears in another block on the quilt.

Approximately forty-five members of the guild worked on the quilt. When their designer friend was suddenly taken ill and passed away in the autumn of 1995, they decided to honor her by giving the quilt to the museum. A lovely inked label on the back of the quilt states that it was donated in memory of Trudy Springer.

Gift of the Waterford Quilters' Guild

VQM LOGO QUILT
1992   44" x 62"

This quilt features the block used to represent the Virginia Quilt Museum on its sign, letterhead, and tote bags. Made by Jackie Kellam of Stephens City, Virginia, the quilt is constructed of six Crab Apple blossom blocks set with a latticed sashing.

The Crab Apple pattern was once showcased in the Nancy Cabot column, a syndicated *Chicago Tribune* column written in the 1930s by Loretta Leitner Rising. The feature was a source of mail-order quilt patterns for women across the country.

The Shenandoah Valley is noted for its apple blossoms, which inspired the selection of this pattern as the museum's logo.

Gift of Jackie Kellam

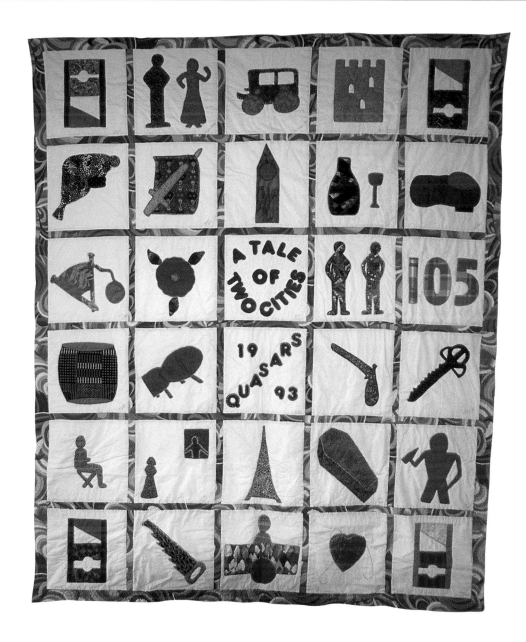

A TALE OF TWO CITIES QUILT

c. 1993   63" x 75"

Since its opening, the Virginia Quilt Museum has included quilts made by young people in every exhibit as examples of our quilting heritage being passed on to the next generation. This is one of three quilts given to the museum by a Tidewater-area schoolteacher. All three were made by her students at Great Neck Middle School in Virginia Beach, Virginia. Each quilt represents a book read in their eighth-grade English class.

In 1993, the students designed blocks

depicting *A Tale of Two Cities*. Using brightly colored fabrics sewn onto muslin backgrounds, they made their blocks, and the teacher joined them together to form the quilt top. The quilt was layered with batting and a back and machine quilted.

Caught in the Act: A Family Apart, made in 1994, and Don Quixote, made in 1993, are the other two student-made quilts that were donated with the Tale of Two Cities.

Gift of Sue Poe

TRIPTYCH/POTTERY IN ANOTHER CONTEXT QUILT

1993   43 1/4" x 70"

This contemporary art quilt was made by Julia E. Pfaff of Richmond, Virginia. The artist divides her time between quilt making and summers as an archaeological illustrator in Greece, Egypt, and Jordan. She incorporates her drawings from the archaeological digs into her quilts.

Julia uses various techniques, such as etching, lithography, and silk screening, to print images of excavated artifacts onto hand-dyed and hand-painted fabrics. The printed fabric is then cut up and reassembled into larger works representing archaeological themes. Julia uses both machine- and hand-piecing methods to assemble her quilt tops; most are then machine-quilted.

The quilt maker states that her work "deals with both narrative and allegorical issues. Man's legacy from the past is manifest in the artifacts, architectural foundations, and ruins left behind. For several months a year I live surrounded by this legacy. My intention in this work is to convey, through the vehicle of archaeological subject, universal themes drawn from the realm of collective experience. I see archaeology's quest for historical and cultural identity as a metaphor for the individual's search for identity. My interest lies in the nexus of the physical and spiritual, the known and the unknown, the found and the sought."

Gift of private donor

SUNSHINE AND SHADOWS AMISH QUILT
1994   41" x 41"

Made in Pennsylvania, this small wall quilt typifies the traditional Amish colors and quilt designs of Lancaster County. The Sunshine and Shadows pattern is also known as Trip around the World.

Quilted with black thread, the center of the piece is covered with a cross-hatch design. Diamond shapes with pumpkin seed motifs within are quilted on the inner border. The outer border is quilted with feather swags.

Gift of Merlyn Hunger

COMMUNITY RESOLUTION QUILT

1996—97   82" x 102"

Each year the city of Harrisonburg, Virginia, welcomes the New Year with its First Night Celebration on December 31. The quilt museum offers the community an opportunity to view the quilts on display and enjoy a featured musi-

cian. In 1996, the theme of the celebration was the diversity of the community, and the museum sponsored the making of a "resolution quilt."

The design is the Courthouse Steps version of the Log Cabin quilt pattern, which

was chosen because Harrisonburg's celebration centers around its courthouse square just before the stroke of midnight. The light strips in this pattern provided space in which revelers could sign their names and write their New Year's resolutions.

The quilt was assembled and tied during the year, and on New Year's Eve 1997 it was displayed at the museum. Many of the hundreds who signed the quilt returned to see it completed and to recall whether or not they had kept their resolutions. The quilt was entered in the International First Night Competition in the spring of 1997 and was one of the top five winners for best idea for the celebration. It inspired other communities to make quilts a part of their festivities.

THE SOWER QUILT

1997   54" x 54"

Made by Sandra Sider of New York, this was the first art quilt given to the museum. When Sandra, who curated an exhibit of quilts from her New York guild for the museum in the spring of 1999, heard that the collection was entirely without contemporary art quilts, she offered the museum a choice of three.

The Sower is a self-portrait sun print created on cotton fabric that was sensitized with cyanotype chemicals. Embellished with painting and embroidery, it is machine quilted.

The artist states that her quilt "celebrates the rebirth and renewal of spring, and of art, as the sower dances from darkness to light."

Gift of Sandra Sider

·THE ANTIQUE SEWING MACHINE ROOM·

O N THE SECOND FLOOR OF THE museum is a display that resulted from an early exhibition featuring antique sewing machines amongst the quilts. After the exhibit closed, visitors continually asked where all the machines had gone. After many inquiries, Mr. Vaughn Simmons, who had loaned most of the machines, was contacted and asked if he would like to exhibit his collection on a regular basis in an upstairs room. Thus the Antique Sewing Machine Room was established.

In it visitors can find early Howe models and numerous Wilcox and Gibbs machines that show the progression from hand-operated models to treadle- and electric-powered ones. A number of different Singer machines are in various types of cases. Many machines have been added as the result of donations to the museum. One is an ornate Singer portable decorated with gold trim. It came from Belgium and was used by the

donor's mother and sisters to make clothes during World War II, all by hand-turning the wheel.

On a side wall, one can find shelves of vintage sewing tools, along with an array of toy sewing machines. One of the favorites of visitors is the "Little Comfort" manufactured by Smith and Egge in the early 1900s. It is a tiny cast-iron sewing machine measuring about seven inches high and six inches wide. It is run by a chain drive and has an automatic tension, a seam guide, and a stitch length regulator.

This room is particularly enjoyed by the men who visit the quilt museum, though everyone seems to delight in its treasures and the fond memories they evoke.

J. KNIGHT

THE VIRGINIA QUILT MUSEUM HAS A SMALL COLLECTION of antique clothing that once was worn by quilters. Visitors enjoy viewing the garments because they offer insight into the daily lives of quilt makers from various time periods.

These three dresses are from the late 1800s and once belonged to Melinda Jane Still Flint (1833–1919), a quilter from West Virginia. The garments were given to the museum by her great-great-granddaughter Allene Blessing, a resident of Harrisonburg.

The pink parasol and child's dress belonged to the Spitzer sisters of Rockingham County, Virginia. The items were donated along with the family quilts by Mary Spitzer Etter. It is believed that Ellen Spitzer might have made the little dress for her daughter, Vernie. Hand sewn, it is made from the "double pink" fabric of the era that was so popular with quilters then and still is today.

·MUSEUM LIBRARY·

THE QUILT MUSEUM'S reference library contains books on every aspect of quilt making, as well as an extensive collection of children's books on quilt-related topics. The majority of the books have been donated to the museum from private collections; others have been purchased through individual contributions.

Thanks to generous donors, the library also houses a collection of vintage quilt pattern books, cardboard quilting templates, and scrapbooks filled with old newspaper clippings relating to quilting, some dating back to the 1920s. Many of the antique patterns have been photocopied and put into binders so that visitors may have access to the designs without disturbing the originals.

One part of the collection is a series of red work patterns that appeared in the *Seattle Star* in the late 1920s and early 1930s. The original scrapbooks, one of which is pictured above, were donated by Jean Knowlton of Gloucester, Virginia, along with more than one hundred cardboard quilting templates. The scrapbooks came from an old family friend, while the "box of patterns" was purchased by the donor at an auction in Homer City, Pennsylvania. The auctioneer held up one of the intricate feather templates and called for bids. Jean bought the whole box for twenty-five cents! Delightful surprises are found on the backs of the patterns as they were cut from old cereal boxes, department store boxes, and puzzle boxes.

·ADDENDUM·

ON MARCH 18, 2000, NATIONAL QUILTING DAY, Senator Kevin Miller and Delegate Glenn Weatherholtz presented the museum with the resolution passed by the members of the Virginia General Assembly "designating the Virginia Quilt Museum in Harrisonburg as the Official Quilt Museum of the Commonwealth."

The Harrisonburg City Council adopted and approved on March 28, 2000, an ordinance gifting the parcel of real estate at 301 South Main Street to the Virginia Quilt Museum.

·APPENDIX·

Applique Pattern: "Open End Signature Wreath"
from the Harrison Family Album Top

Add 1/4" seam allowances to all pieces.
Enlarge design 158% on copier to achieve original size.

Finished block measures 15" sq.

Ink Signature and Date in Center of Wreath

Applique Pattern: "Tulip Basket"
from the Greene Family Album Quilt

Finished block measures 17" sq.
Enlarge design 220% on copier to achieve original size.

Small circles on basket are done in reverse applique.
Add 1/4" seam allowances to all pieces.
R= Red solid
T= Tan solid

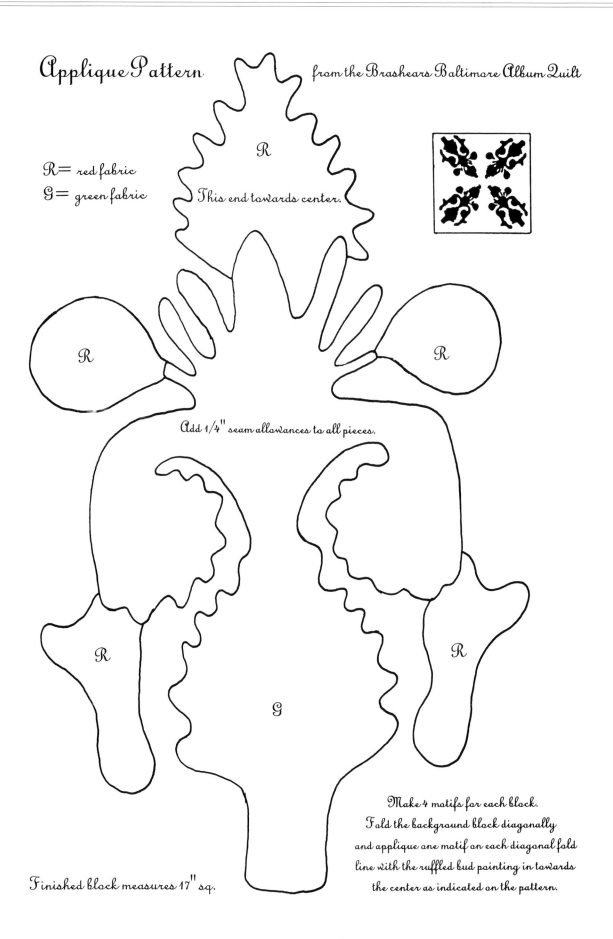

Applique Pattern   from the Brashears Baltimore Album Quilt

R= red fabric
G= green fabric

R

This end towards center.

R   R

Add 1/4" seam allowances to all pieces.

R   R

G

Make 4 motifs for each block.
Fold the background block diagonally
and applique one motif on each diagonal fold
line with the ruffled bud pointing in towards
Finished block measures 17" sq.   the center as indicated on the pattern.

Pieced Pattern: "Wagon Wheel"
from the Wagon Wheel Quilt

Assemble in units as shown below:

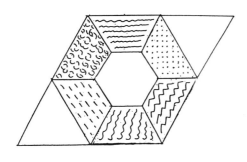 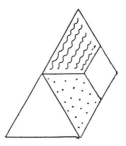

Block Unit   Side Unit

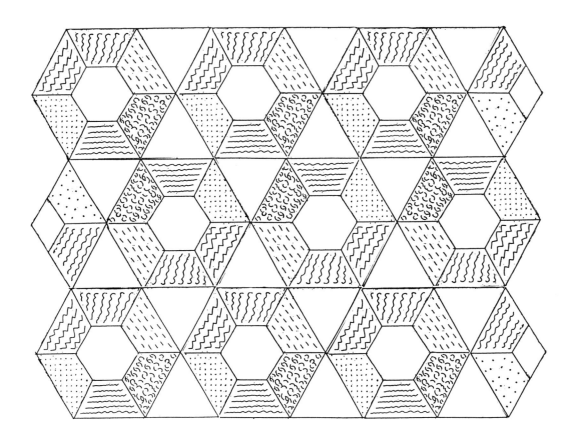

Templates for "Wagon Wheel" Quilt

This quilt pattern was originally made using plain feed sacks
for the background pieces and assorted 1930's printed fabrics for the wheels.

Add 1/4" seam allowances to all pieces.

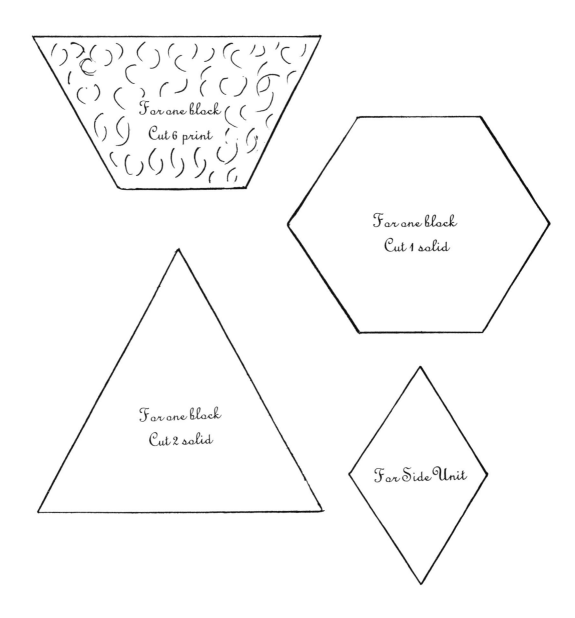

For one block

Cut 6 print

For one block
Cut 1 solid

For one block
Cut 2 solid

For Side Unit

Crazy Patch Patterns
from "Mother's Blessing Crazy Quilt"

Add 1/4" seam allowances to all pieces.

"Purse of Thrift"

"Broom of Neatness"

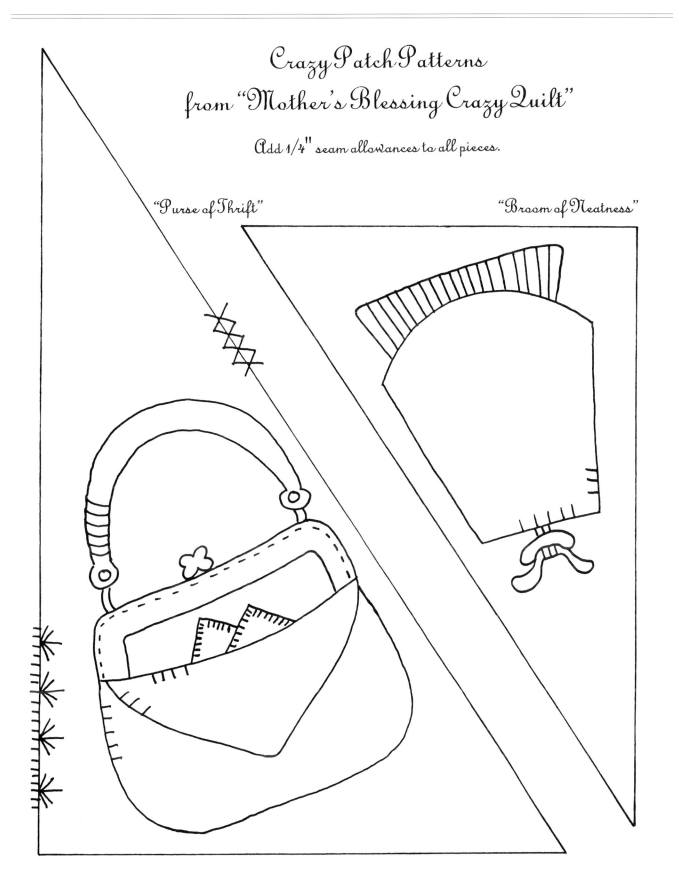

The purse handle is formed with satin stitches, as well as the broom bristles and handle.

Buttonhole and other fancy stitches are indicated where they are used.

Red Work Doll Quilt Patterns

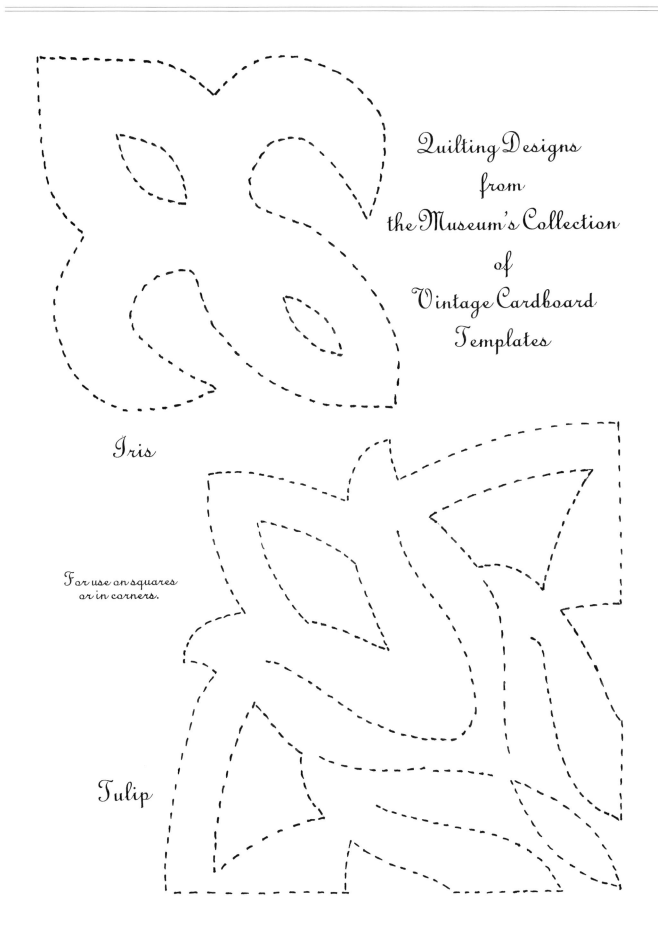

Quilting Designs
from
the Museum's Collection
of
Vintage Cardboard
Templates

Iris

For use on squares
or in corners.

Tulip

Quilting Designs from the Museum's
Collection of Vintage Cardboard
Templates

Flower/Star motifs

Pieced Pattern: "Arrow"
from the Arrow Quilt

The finished block measures 10" square.

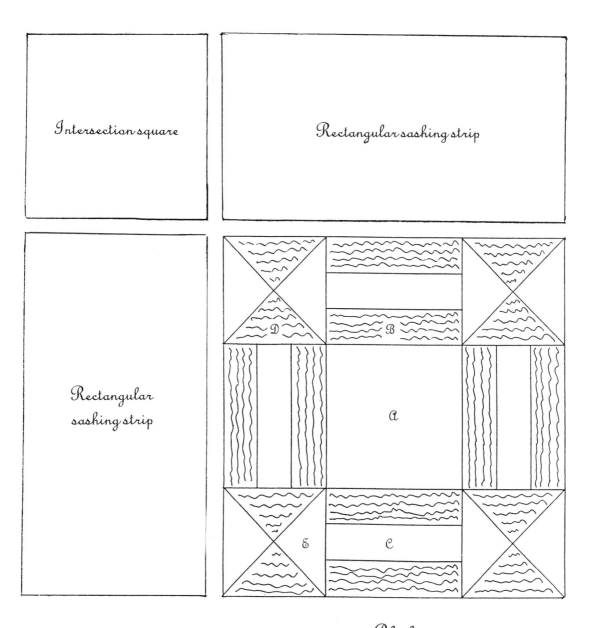

Intersection square

Rectangular sashing strip

Rectangular sashing strip

D

B

A

E

C

Block

"Arrow" Pattern Pieces

Add 1/4" seam allowances to all pieces.
For one block, cut the number of pieces indictated:

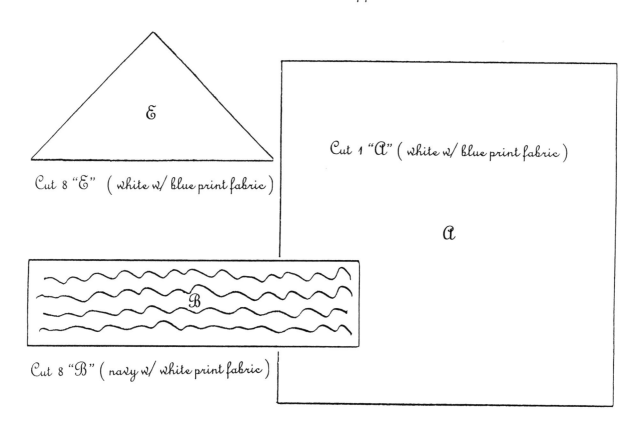

Cut 8 "E" (white w/ blue print fabric)

Cut 1 "A" (white w/ blue print fabric)

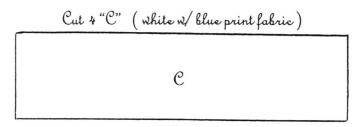

Cut 8 "B" (navy w/ white print fabric)

Cut 4 "C" (white w/ blue print fabric)

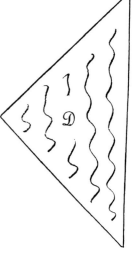

Cut sashing units with 1/4" seam allowances added:
Intersection Squares 5 ½" x 5 ½" white w/ blue
Rectangular Strips 5 ½" x 10 ½" pink print

Finished sizes for sashing units:
Intersection squares are 5" x 5" each
Rectangular sashing strips are 5" x 10" each

Cut 8 "D" (navy w/ white print fabric)

·INDEX·